For Patricia and Jacqueline

My Mothers

ONE TRUE REFLECTION

Transformation into Truth

RICHARD SYKES

CONTENTS

PART 3

LOST IN THE ILLUSION

PART 4

LIFE IS A MIRROR

PART 5

PEELING AWAY THE LAYERS

PART 6

THE REUNION

INTRODUCTION

I once read an interesting article about a science class in which the students were studying metamorphosis. They collected a caterpillar cocoon to observe its transformation into a butterfly. The caterpillar had been in its cocoon for months. Then one day with the aid of a stethoscope, the students heard the noise of the butterfly struggling to break free from its old home. With excitement and meticulous care, the students made an incision at the end of the cocoon, allowing the butterfly to crawl out. It began to sluggishly unfold its misshapen wings that could not flutter as butterfly wings should. It attempted to move them many times, but they would not function properly. After some time, the butterfly died as a weak and paralyzed creature without the strength to survive. In their naivety, the students did not realise that their efforts to help and assist with the caterpillar's transformation had caused it irreparable harm. When they assisted the butterfly's painless release from its cocoon, they deprived it of the necessary struggle and suffering that would have strengthened its wings. It never got the growth it needed, to not only survive, but flourish as a butterfly.

This begs the questions, is suffering necessary? Yes and no. I see suffering as a bit of a paradox. It is necessary until it is unnecessary. The butterfly uses the strain and stress to transform and knows at which point it has suffered enough as it breaks free from its cocoon. As for us humans, we get lost in our suffering as we endlessly search for a way out.

We try countless ways to avoid feeling any pain, and in the process, create and perpetuate it. Many of us do not even realise that we are suffering or going through a transformational process, so we stay bewildered by how difficult life can be.

What is suffering? Suffering is the resistance against change and being ourselves. One of our greatest fears is being who we truly are. So, we shy away from showing our light, and instead choose to hide in the darkness. We then feel the pain of not being who we are and lack the courage to show ourselves through the burden of the past that we carry around with us. We grow to believe that we are our past and that it is hindering our ability to be who we truly are. The truth is that your past, no matter how dark it may have been, can be seen as a blessing.

My name is Richard Sykes. When I was four years old I witnessed my mother being murdered. I'm going to tell you about my life and journey so that when you read the rest of this book you will know that you are not limited by your past; in fact, quite the opposite. We can use a seemingly tragic or painful past as the fuel to transcend our limited perception of who we think we are.

I was born in 1982 in Huddersfield, West Yorkshire, England. When I was 18 months old, my dad, who was an engineer, got a job in New York, and the plan was that we would all follow him in six months. But my parent's relationship was unravelling and being apart from each other for six months only made things worse. While my dad was away, my mum became close to a man named Shaun Clarke, who quickly showed himself to be jealous and obsessive. He did things like spying on my mum through his binoculars, and, on one occasion, threatened her with a knife. Despite this, my mum continued spending time with Shaun, until my dad returned to the UK and took us all back to America with him.

After several months, my mother brought my brother and I back to the UK, and we all moved in with her sister. Next time my mum went to America to see my father, she left us in the UK to stay at my aunt's, and when she came back, she told us that the marriage was over.

My mum started seeing Shaun again. When me and my brother were in bed, we could hear Shaun shouting at our mum, even hitting her. My brother would lock us in our bedroom for protection, and sometimes we'd sleep in the same bed to feel safe. We would occasionally stay over at our aunt's, and we'd lock ourselves in our bedroom there too.

Finally, my mum gathered the courage to tell Shaun to leave. He was banished, but he did not go away. Evenings were spent watching movies, trying to drown out the sound of Shaun shouting abuse through the letter box. At night-times, we'd all sleep-in mum's bed to keep each other safe. We didn't feel any safer during the day. Once, Shaun chased us all through a housing estate. We were running down a hill when he threw a plastic bag filled with bottles at us. It smashed and broken glass hit my ankle, opening a deep cut. As the blood poured out, my mum frantically knocked on a stranger's door for help. An Asian lady brought us inside and placed my bleeding foot in a bucket.

Shaun's erratic and threatening behavior was all the more confusing for me because at times he could be very nice. I remember him taking me out shooting his air rifle and painting my toy truck.

One night, Shaun managed to get into the house. Upstairs, my brother and I listened to the shouting and fighting going on below and becoming frightened by the sound of our mother's mounting distress. Me and my brother decided to creep downstairs to find out what was happening. Peering through the half-open sitting room door, we silently watched Shaun Clarke murder our mother. He strangled her. When he spotted us watching him, he slammed the door so hard it took one of my toe nails off as it ran over my foot. My brother and I ran as fast as we could back upstairs and hid until the police finally arrived, called by a man who saw our mother's dead body through the window. The police eventually coaxed us back downstairs by calling through the letter box. They took us away and we stayed with our aunt.

I was only a little kid and didn't really understand what had happened, or where our mum had gone. I remember going back home to collect one of my toys and seeing black finger prints all over the house. This tragedy sent out a shockwave in all directions, affecting everybody it touched in different ways. My father did not come rushing back. In fact, he turned up on the day of the court case to determine who would gain custody of my brother and I, but he was late for the hearing. My aunt was granted custody; she became and still is my mother. But to avoid any confusion I will refer to her as my aunt.

Shaun was tracked down and arrested and convicted of murder. Twenty years later, not long after his release from prison, he stalked a beautiful blonde woman, broke into her house, and stabbed her to death. He then walked into some nearby woods and hanged himself.

After the murder of my mother, my brother and I were taken to have sessions with child psychologists, to help us recover from the trauma and loss. In our new home, living with our aunt, we became, and still are, very close. We shared a bedroom until I was about 14, and I would still occasionally climb into his bed if I were having nightmares.

Our aunt raised us as if we were her own children, and as a family we went everywhere and did everything together. I learned many valuable lessons from my aunt; like how to never give up. My aunt is one of the strongest women I know. Given the circumstances of her loosing her sister and best friend she still managed to raise me, my brother, and her daughter on her own.

Growing up we rarely spoke about my mother and the tragedy that took place. The pain of what happened seemed to over shadow the memory of her. Understandably, my mother's murder deeply affected those closest to her, but the lack of communication deeply frustrated me.

It was over ten years before my dad tried to reconnect with us. I was 15. My aunt respected the fact that he was our father and gave him permission to come and see us. As he came to visit us at home and walked through the door to the living room, I felt no connection to him. He was simply a stranger coming to visit for the first time. Several outings with him proved that it was not going to work. Eventually his visits faded, and we never saw him again. By that time, I was 16. I felt like I didn't care about anyone or anything. I started doing drugs. I was smoking cannabis, then moved on to ecstasy and amphetamines.

I left home and moved in with a friend called Nigel. Nigel's house was the party house, and it is where I dropped my first E. We had party after party and did nothing but take drugs and drink. It was all I wanted to do. I spent all my money on drugs. I lost a lot of weight as I did not have any money to eat. To feed myself, I took to walking into the nearest supermarket with a bag, filling it full of food and walking back out. I started to realise that things were getting out of control when I had not slept for four days. I was losing all empathy and compassion. I was oblivious to how my behavior was affecting those who cared for me, as the only thing I cared about was getting high.

I could see that my life was quickly heading down the toilet, so I decided to join the British Army. It seemed like a good plan. Back in 1999, the British Army was only involved in NATO peace-keeping and no actual wars. So, at the age of 17, I became a soldier. My plan was to spend five years in the army, which would give me enough time to get my life together and then leave to find a job back in civilian life. Just over one year later, I was stationed in London when someone told us to turn on the TV. In shock, I watched as the devastation unfolded in New York. Planes crashed into towers that I had stood inside as a child. Only a few days later all the green military vehicles were painted a sandy color – an early indication that we were going to war. Luckily for me I was never sent to Afghanistan or Iraq.

My time in the army may have saved me from the life I was living in Huddersfield, but I had stepped into a world that was not much better. The army instilled regimentation and control, which for me and many others led to aggression. This also stirred up and exaggerated all the unresolved anger already inside me. Not knowing how to deal with these emotions meant I would go out drinking and fighting, and trouble became a good friend of mine. On New Year's Eve 2004, I was on leave at home in Huddersfield and out drinking with a friend. Tanked up with alcohol and filled with anger I attracted the usual trouble and ended up having a fight with two men. This resulted in me spending the night in the police station, and nearly going to jail. Who was this horrible person I had become? I knew that if I stayed in the army, that person would not change, he would become worse. So, in 2006, I left the British Army after serving six years, vowing that I would get my life together.

Not long after leaving the army, I bumped into my friend Nigel. He was now using heroin, and a few years later was found dead in his bathtub. This gave me a glimpse of what could have happened to me if I had carried on down the same path. I felt driven to start creating change in my life. I quickly became financially successful, working in the sales industry, selling anything from double glazed windows, to solar panels. Three years after leaving the British Army at the age of 26 It seemed I had achieved what I believed would bring me the happiness I was looking for. I was earning a good amount of money, had a nice car, apartment, and beautiful girlfriend. But something was clearly out of balance as I started waking up in the mornings feeling fatigued. I kept going nonetheless, until one evening when everything came to a dramatic halt. I was out with my girlfriend Lisa and friends, when suddenly, I felt like I was going to faint. I stumbled out of the restaurant and collapsed onto the pavement. My entire left side became numb and my heart was racing. I thought I was having a stroke. Lisa quickly phoned a taxi and took me to hospital, where the doctors hooked me up to machines, and checked my heart rate and blood pressure before revealing that I had had a panic attack. "Panic attack? Not me!" I thought.

I woke up the next day with a migraine that lasted for six months, and I was so fatigued that I could barely get myself out of bed in the mornings. When I did manage to scrape myself out of bed I would feel the same level of tiredness as I had when I went to bed. My memory and focus were so impaired that, when driving, I'd occasionally forget where I was going, and have to pull the car over and sit for ten minutes to remember my destination. The doctors diagnosed me with Chronic Fatigue Syndrome and tried to palm me off with anti-depressants. They also told me it was incurable and that I would have it for the rest of my life. I sat in my apartment and started to ponder over my life. I had everything I believed would bring me happiness, but I was ill, insecure, and certainly not happy.

I found myself reading books on anything that involved self-healing and happiness. I became obsessed and read book after book on the power of the mind, meditation, philosophy, and spirituality. This was a whole new world to me, but I felt like I'd found something incredibly interesting and true. I accumulated a wealth of knowledge and began putting it into practice. I started to meditate, eat healthily and exercise. I also started to question my life and all that I believed would make me happy. I wanted to know where happiness and health truly came from. I knew the life that I had created was not giving me what I believed it would. In fact, it was giving me the opposite. I felt I needed to detach from my environment to give myself the time and space to discover what I was searching for. So, Lisa and I sold all our belongings, quit our jobs, and decided to travel the world for 12 months.

Our first stop was Thailand, where I decided to propose to Lisa. We had been together for five years and I thought it was the right thing to do. She said yes! We travelled through Thailand, Cambodia and Vietnam and I spent some time alone in Peru. I arrived back in Thailand to meet Lisa and we travelled down to a small island called Koh Phangan. It was there that I discovered my passion for helping others. It began when I spotted a flyer for a course in something called Theta Healing. Like Hypnotherapy, it enables us to find and change subconscious beliefs that are creating unwanted life situations. When I saw the poster, I felt like my cells started vibrating with excitement shouting at me to do the course, so I signed up right away.

After the course, I knew this was what I wanted to do with my life. I had never felt so sure about anything. My intention was so strong that, just two hours after finishing the course, I had a random conversation with a man, gave him a free session, he turned out to be the owner of a healing retreat and he offered me a job on the spot. Over the next four months I worked non-stop. There were a queue of people wanting sessions from me, and it seemed very easy and natural to assist others. After spending four months on this magical island my visa eventually expired, and we had to keep moving.

After our time in Thailand, we continued our travels, flying to New Zealand, then Australia, and the United States, landing in California. By this time six months had passed, and our money was running low. Lisa wanted to volunteer and learn permaculture, and I decided to go to a meditation retreat in Nevada City. My health seemed to be improving, but I knew I needed deeper healing. Most of my time was spent in meditation, which enabled me to reflect on myself and my life. I was changing so fast that it felt hard to keep up. All the ideas I had based on what I believed would make me happy were being peeled away.

This rapid change made me question everything in my life, including my relationship with Lisa, the person that I thought I wanted to marry. I became distant from her. She tried to salvage our relationship, but I pushed her away. My whole life was being shaken up. I felt lost and alone, and unable to communicate what I was feeling, certain that nobody would understand what I was going through. But then, at the meditation retreat, I met and instantly clicked with Frank from Texas. I told him some of my experiences and he could relate to them. This gave me a huge lift and I started spending time with Frank and his friend Chelsea, also from Texas. We all understood each other and supported one another's journey and vison, for the first time in my life, I felt truly seen and heard. We three became close, and I started to develop feelings for Chelsea, as she did for me. Lisa decided to travel up to Canada to pursue her passion for permaculture. I did not go with her.

Instead, at the end of the month-long retreat, Frank, Chelsea, and I left and drove to a spiritual hot spot called Mt Shasta. We camped out most nights and connected with amazing people. It felt great to see how many people were on a similar path to me, and I no longer felt alone and alienated. I was experiencing something I had never really had before – honest, open, and meaningful communication with other people who were seeing the world as I was starting to see it.

One day I decided to visit a coffee shop in the town where we were camping. As I sat down to drink my tea, I spotted a monk at a table across from me. I was feeling confused about my situation. I was engaged to Lisa but was also in love with Chelsea. As I looked up, I noticed the monk was staring right at me. He called to me, inviting me to his table. As I sat down, he looked me in the eyes and, in broken English, said, "You have women trouble." Before I could reply, he continued, "You need to decide what you want for your life and who you are becoming as a person. You are a crystal ball, which has a little dust on it, you need to blow off the dust, and you shall discover who you are." This man had peered into my soul. I later found out that he was an important monk from Thailand, whom people would wait up to five years to spend ten minutes with. I left the coffee shop, walked round the side of the building into the car park, and burst into tears. I had a loving fiancé in Canada, and I was busy falling in love with Chelsea, and she with me. I felt like I was in a bubble that had just burst. I took the monk's advice and did what I felt was the right thing to do. I told Chelsea that I needed to leave to go to Lisa in Canada. Even though I knew that I could end up alone, I felt at peace, knowing that whatever happened would be the right thing.

When I met with Lisa, we agreed that our relationship was no longer working, and we would be better to end it. Even though we still loved each other, we honoured the fact that we wanted different things. We wanted each other to be happy, and that meant letting each other go.

Lisa stayed in Canada, and I decided to make my way back down to California. I was not sure what I would do, or where to go once I arrived back in California. But I trusted life to take me where I needed to be. I stayed overnight at a hostel in Canada before making my way back down to California. When I arrived in the room that I was sharing with around six other people, I became friendly with a man named Beni from Germany. I told him that I was planning to make my way back down to California, and to my surprise, so was he. Beni said he was thinking of buying a cheap van that he could use for transport and to sleep in. He said that it would be nice to have company, so we agreed, after having known each other for just over one hour that we would spend the next three months together. Because I had already visited many amazing parts of California with Frank and Chelsea I was able to introduce Beni to these places. We spent some time in Mt Shasta and connected with many amazing and interesting people, and then worked our way down to San Diego, stopping at many beautiful places along the way. My time with Beni was magical and the number of syncronicities we experienced together would be just too many to mention. Three months later I arrived in San Diego. My plan was to sell the van, split the money with Beni and have a little money to come back to the UK with. I listed the van on a local website and met with somebody who wanted to buy it. Upon his inspection though, he discovered the van was damaged and needed some costly repairs. I drove the van to a garage and received an estimate that was more than what I was planning to sell the van for. I ended up practically giving the van away. I then traveled down to Los Angeles by coach to catch my flight back to the UK.

After spending 12 months traveling the world I was back in the UK: jobless, single, homeless, and broke. From the outside, it looked like I had nothing, when in fact I had more than ever before. I carried inside me a new perspective of myself and the world. I was beginning to know and feel who I was and who I was not. My family understandably found it difficult to adjust to the new me or understand what had happened. And it was impossible for me to put my experiences into words. I had to understand that they did not understand who I had become.

It was extremely difficult for me to re-connect back into my home environment. I felt like a stranger among my family and friends, and so I became a bit of a recluse. The type of open and meaningful conversations that I had had on my travels were few and far between. I felt like I was closing and choosing not to truly show myself like I had when I was traveling.

I rented a room at a friend's house and decided to get a job back in the sales industry, selling solar panels. Sales came very naturally to me, and so I thought I could use this to create some stability in my life. But it seemed that life had other plans and was pushing me towards following through with the intention I made in Thailand. I had five different sales jobs in the same number of months. No matter how hard I worked something always seemed to sabotage my ability to integrate myself back into this old way of living. I started to pay attention to life and see where I was being encouraged to focus my energies. I decided to take a course in another healing modality called Emotional Freedom Technique. My health was improving, and it made sense for me to keep the momentum going and help myself as I was helping others.

I emailed the trainer of the course, Karl Dawson and explained my situation plus a little bit about my journey. A little later I received a phone call from Karl and we chatted for hours. He had also spent time in Thailand and been on a similar journey to me. He offered me a place on his course, and to teach me his own powerful healing modality called Matrix Re-Imprinting. During the course and whilst using this technique on myself and others, I was amazed at how quickly ailments and long-standing physical pain would vanish. It was now becoming very clear to me how much the conditioning from our past severely limits who we are. I knew that this course would further enable me to, not only finally heal myself, but to help others heal.

Not long after the EFT course I unexpectedly received a phone call from a sales company in Indonesia. They had seen my CV online and wanted me to work for them. I rejected their offer and explained that I was fully focused on my healing work. A few days later I received another phone call, this time it was a man named Clive, the owner of the company. He expressed his desire for me to work for them. Again, I rejected the offer. I then received a third phone call, again from Clive. He explained that they would pay for my flight to Indonesia, put me up in a fancy hotel, take care of my expenses and pay me a good salary. I felt conflicted with my decision. I knew that my passion and calling was to work with other people, but felt like I was back in an environment that I did not want to be in. I asked Clive to give me a few days to think it over, he gave me 24 hours to make my decision, and explained it would be the last opportunity. 24 hours later, he called. He said I could give it six months and if I did not like the job, I could leave. I thought that, in the worst-case scenario, I would have a long holiday to Indonesia and be able to use the money to support me doing what I wanted to do. So, I accepted the job and within a few weeks I was at the company being trained. But, when I met Clive, it turned out he'd been making false promises. I had been lied to about the job and was now stuck in Indonesia with no money. I did not know what to do but knew I had to leave. Suddenly out of the blue I received an email from the owner of the healing retreat I was working at in Koh Phangan. He asked where I was, they were short staffed and needed more practitioners to help out. I was just over the water in Indonesia! I instantly replied to the email and caught a flight the next morning. I was back in Thailand following through with my intention. Even though the job in Indonesia did not turn out to be what they said it was, it did not matter, because it turned out to be the reason I was close to the place I needed to be.

Back at the retreat, I gave session after session to anybody who needed assistance. Giving so many sessions gave me insights into how we are all identified with a limited and false self, the ego. I then started to hear "diss-identification" ringing in my ears. I knew that the way to true happiness would come when we diss-identify with whom we have been conditioned to think we are. Identifying with all our past conditioning brings the pain. This made it obvious that to diss-identify meant freedom. I could then clearly see how I had been identified with my past pain, and how it was blocking my ability to be healthy and truly happy. So, I decided to lock myself away in my little beach hut and I spent the next three months in meditation, facing and working through the darkness within. This sped up my recovery until I was fatigue-free and healthy again. I could not stop the momentum that had been created through my relentless search for better health. I felt that something had taken over and was guiding me.

One morning whilst in meditation, I felt a strong push to start teaching what I had learned. I was giving many one-to-one sessions, but I knew I needed to start speaking to more people. I felt resistance and fear rise inside of me, but I knew it was time for me to start sharing my truth. I gave my first ever workshop in front of 25 people, it felt more like 250 people, I was so nervous. However, a couple of minutes into the workshop, a feeling of peace washed over me, as though I was being guided. It was like I was being spoken through. I was amazed to see how, every time I was asked a question, an answer would arise from within and pop out of my mouth. I was not having to think of what to say, I was just saying it. After the workshop I felt euphoric, so I carried on hosting them, and listening to where life was guiding me, and more importantly to what it was teaching me. I also brought this guidance into my sessions and started working intuitively, which allowed the sessions to go much deeper, creating better results.

Something special was happening to me that I could not put into words. I was being guided by life and having many profound experiences that would take me deeper into my true state of my being. I carried on meditating and letting go of the limiting concepts of who I believed I was, and, for the first time in a long while, I started to feel at peace.

After spending another nine months on this beautiful island, sharing and deepening my truth, it was time for me to leave. Even though I was reluctant to go, I knew it was time to keep moving. A friend of mine had moved to Berlin and shared with me how amazing it was. She explained how it was creative and liberal and felt that what I had to offer would fit perfectly with the kind of people that lived there. I knew that I wanted to keep the momentum going with my workshops and private coaching sessions, so I decided to move to Berlin. I combined all the different healing techniques I had learned over the six-year period since leaving the UK, into an intuitive coaching practice. Berlin is a liberal and creative city so what I was offering was well received. After being in Berlin for close to one year I had created a steady income and was about to move into my own apartment. It was November 2015 and I did not have any plans for Christmas, but I had stayed in contact with a beautiful lady I met in Koh Phangan called Anna. Over the space of the twelve months we had stayed in contact through video calls, we had developed a deep connection. I decided to fly over and spend one week with her in Sweden. One week turned into one month, and after spending a lovely Christmas in Sweden it was time for me to return to Berlin. Anna came to visit me in Berlin not long after I had arrived back, and then flew back home to Sweden. Then around one month after Anna had been back in Sweden, she called me to share some exciting news. She was pregnant.

We spent some time discussing the logistics of how we would make this work. Anna felt it would be best for me to move to Sweden and live with her. But I was on the verge on moving into my own apartment and felt that all the ground work I had put into my time in Berlin would have been for nothing. I had regular workshops running and an increasing number of clients to coach. I also had to appreciate that Anna had a job and a life in Sweden. After several lengthy discussions we decided that me moving to Sweden would be the better option. In February 2016 I packed my bags and said my goodbyes to Berlin.

Upon my arrival to Sweden I had to register with the local authorities to be able to live and work. This process seemed to take forever, and I had to jump through many hoops for eight months. I was still coaching a handful of people online and that created a little bit of money. But Anna was supporting us both, she was pregnant, and this added to my frustration. I had to swallow my pride and keep going with the flow, knowing that I would soon be registered to work.

Then, on August 2016 our beautiful baby girl was born. She was screaming, and the midwife placed her into my arms. She was laid on my bare chest and immediately stopped crying. No sooner after she had stopped crying, floods of tears came streaming down my face. I had never felt such a pure loving bond like this before.

Several months after our daughter was born, I received my identification number which entitled me to start working. Anna suggested that I consider getting a job as a Personal Assistant to create some money. I initially snubbed the idea, but after some consideration I decided to explore any available positions. Anna joked that it would be funny if I found somebody to care for who lived just down the road. Sure enough there was a job listed for an elderly Asian man who had had a stroke and needed caring for during the day and night. He was a 5 minutes' walk away. I applied for the job and an interview was created. Upon my arrival for the interview I met Zal, the man that I would be caring for, and his lovely Swedish wife Brittinger. I instantly felt at home. Brittinger was very open minding and spiritual. I sat and spoke with Zal and Brittinger for around one hour. I met their beautiful children and we all seemed to get along just fine. Several days later, I received news that I had indeed got the position as Zal's Personal Assistant. My plan was to work part time for Zal alongside my workshops and coaching. But after several months I found myself working full time with little time to spare to focus on anything else. I embraced this new experience and realised that life was teaching me a valuable lesson. Having to shower and feed an adult man cultivated humility within me. I knew that my new position was not just about creating stability for my new little family. Every day spent with Zal and his wife taught me valuable lessons about myself.

Months passed by, and before I knew it, I had been living in Sweden for 2 years. As much as I loved my Personal Assistance work I felt the urge and calling to focus more on my workshops and coaching. One morning after I had finished feeding Zal his breakfast, we both pulled one of Brittinger's angel cards. I cannot remember what card Zal pulled, but my card said, "career change". My feelings and intuition had been confirmed. I spoke with Anna and shared that I felt it was time for me to fully focus on my calling again. Anna was understandably concerned that I would not be able to provide for our family. But I knew in my heart it was time for me to leave and honor my calling. So, I spoke with Brittinger and Zal to share the news that I would be leaving, and they both understood and supported my decision. Just when I had become comfortable and a little complacent with my life, big changes were on the horizon again.

Since the birth of my daughter my relationship with Anna had not been the same. I had become a shell of my former self and started to severally neglect myself. I had taken on a role and a personality that was not me, and gradually who I was took a back seat. I felt like an outsider looking in on somebody else's family. I was not being who I knew I was or doing what I wanted to do.

I would wake up in the middle of the night, unable to sleep, feeling like my entire body was on fire. Some nights I would not sleep at all until bedtime became the worst part of the day. I was suffering with chronic stress, but as all of this was going on, I did not discuss it with Anna or anybody else and chose to suffer in silence. My pride was getting in the way, and I would throw myself back into my relationship with Anna, trying to make it work for the sake of our daughter. But no matter how hard I tried to make our relationship work it was clearly not meant to be.

Anna and I agreed that something needed to change. We did not want our relationship to negatively effect our daughter. I tried everything I could to salvage our relationship and to somehow get it back to what it was when we first met. But my efforts did not work, and it became more evident that the only way we all would be happy was if myself and Anna separated. But it was not that simple, as I would not only be leaving Anna, I would be leaving my daughter too.

I started to think about my father and the mistakes he made when I was a child. I remembered that as a child I swore that when I had my own children I would never make the same mistakes that he had made. This deep-rooted vow made me cling onto a relationship that was clearly broken. I was terrified of letting go, and I started to suffer as a consequence. My health became even worse and at times I felt like I was having a heart attack. I was overcome with fear and felt deep despair just at the thought of leaving my daughter. I knew in my heart that if I stayed things would only become worse. I had to listen to my heart and make the hardest decision I've ever had to make in my life. To leave my daughter. I broke the news to Anna that I would be leaving and started looking for an apartment I could rent close by.

Anna was due to go away on holiday with our daughter for ten days. I initially felt I could use this time to get my head straight and know where I was going to go, and what I was going to do. The day arrived for Anna and my daughter to leave on their holiday. I walked them to the bus stop and felt myself welling up with deep sadness. I tried to hold it together for my daughter and remind myself that I was making the right decision, but I could not hold back the tears. I said goodbye to Anna and my daughter knowing I would not be at home when they arrived back. I felt crippled with fear, sadness and confusion, unsure what I would do or where I would go.

I called the local housing office to enquire about the possibility of finding myself a new home. They explained that I would have to wait up to seven years before I would be eligible for my own apartment. I travelled to the closest city to investigate my options. I was met with the same challenge. Again, I felt confused and did not know what to do. The next day I woke to an empty house and a horrible feeling of dread in my stomach. I decided to go for a walk to allow this feeling to be processed and bumped into an elderly lady that lived in the area. Eleanor and I had become friends and would sometimes go for walks and chat. Eleanor would usually do most of the talking and I would appreciate her life stories. She said she felt comfortable around me and that she could tell me anything. During our walk Eleanor immediately sensed that something was not quite right and asked what was wrong. I explained my situation and that I had to leave my relationship but was unsure where to go. Eleanor did not say much, and I did not expect her to. I changed the subject to keep our conversation light and offered to cook some lunch for us both. She agreed, but only if we could eat our lunch in her garden. After we had finished eating, I used her bathroom. I felt so confused and lost that my head was spinning. I got down on my knees and prayed. "Please give me some guidance! Where would you have me go? What would you have me do?" I then came back to sit with Eleanor in the sun. She looked right at me and said "You need to go back to the UK" I instantly felt relief wash over me and burst into tears. I knew what she was saying was true. My prayer had been answered. Eleanor was the angel life presented me within my time of need, to point me in the right direction. And little did I know that I was about to meet two more angels that would virtually save my life.

I knew I had to leave Sweden and go back to the UK. I was still unsure where I would go, once I arrived. One night just before I fell asleep, I saw an image of two people I had been coaching. Michelle and David had contacted me through a YouTube video I had posted. I ended up coaching them for around six months, and afterwards we stayed in contact, and as good friends. During one of our conversations they could see that I was not my usual self and I told them my relationship with Anna was not going well. Their reply was that if I ever were to come back to the UK and needed a place to stay, I would be welcome at their home. At that point, I did not think I would be leaving Anna or Sweden, but I shared my appreciation and agreed that I would take them up on their offer if the opportunity ever arose. I was now about to come back to the UK and I knew that life was guiding me to accept the offer, made by Michelle and David. Without any hesitation I messaged them and explained my situation, sharing with them that I would be coming back to the UK. They replied instantly saying that I was more that welcome to come and stay with them. However due to unforeseen circumstances I found myself without money to pay for a flight.

I was in the same situation as the one when I arrived back in the UK after traveling the world. Again, I would be homeless, jobless, broke and single. What lesson was life trying to teach me? I decided to pull one of my angel cards and received the card "trust". I was being called to trust myself. I knew in my heart it was time for me to share my gifts with the world, and that everything I had been through was for a reason. It was time for me to take a leap of faith into the unknown. I made a vow that once I arrived back in the UK, I would finish writing this book and do everything I could to be the best father for my daughter. I could see how life had created this situation for me to take a leap of faith, and trust that everything would work out. I then received a message from Michelle and David offering to pay for my flight back to the UK. I accepted their offer and booked a flight to leave the following week. The next seven days were the darkest days of my life. Even though I felt some relief knowing where I was going to go, I still felt deep sadness and grief over leaving my daughter.

As each day passed, I felt more fear and sadness come to the surface, like I was surrounded by a cloud of darkness. Some evenings my entire body would contract and the veins in my left arm would protrude. "This is it" I would think to myself. There seemed to be a force inside of me that was terrified of letting go. Then when the day arrived for me to leave Sweden, I froze with fear. I did not want to leave my baby girl. In my heart I knew that the only way myself and Anna could raise our daughter in a healthy way would be if we did it separately. I had to remind myself why I was leaving and chose to focus on the bigger picture. I was leaving my daughter so that she could be happy. This did not help the despair I was feeling. I took a deep breath, and with the pain of leaving my daughter in my heart, I left Sweden.

The temperate was still extremely high, and I was still very weak. I was carrying my backpack and another bag on my front, trying to walk in the shade to avoid the intense heat. I jumped on the bus and arrived at the train station just in time for my train to the airport. Upon arrival to the airport I felt the heat starting to drain the little energy I had. My entire body started to feel red hot and my heart began to race. When I eventually got onto my flight, I felt a mixture of grief and relief.

Upon my arrival to the UK I was met by David. He picked me up from the airport and drove us both to his beautiful home in Lancashire. I was greeted by Michelle who instantly made me feel welcome and commented on how thin I looked. I had indeed lost a lot of weight due to stress. "Don't worry! I'll fatten you up" said Michelle. And she did just that. I was blessed to be moved into my own little apartment situated on the side of their home. Little did I know that I would not be there alone. Their pet dog was heavily pregnant and delivered what initially looked like nine black slugs. These little black slugs grew into nine beautiful Labrador puppies. The puppies and their mother were kept in the living room of the apartment I was living in. I would get up in the morning and help to clean up any mess they had made, and to feed them.

Over the next eight weeks I naturally fell into the role of puppy caretaker, whilst Michelle and David provided everything I needed to get me back on my feet. Michelle and David also provided me with emotional support and helped me remember the importance of speaking and sharing my truth. The two people that I coached became my mentors.

Slowly my strength increased, and I started to give workshops in a local center, and private coaching sessions. However, the distance from my daughter was starting to take its toll. I felt a heaviness inside that developed into a dark depression and anxiety. I also felt distant from aunt who did not understand my decision to leave my daughter, or the path that I was on. I was not communicating with her clearly due to the state I was in. I felt a strong fear of loss and distanced myself for most of my friends and family.

I started to feel the same alienation when arriving back to the UK after traveling the world. Suicidal thoughts would pass through my mind. I felt like I was sinking into a dark hole, and every time I tried to take action and pull myself out, I would be pulled back into the abyss. The separation from my daughter was triggering deep healing to help me purge my deep-rooted childhood trauma. I knew the only way I could move forwards was to face my deep-rooted unresolved pain head on. I was hit with a tidal wave of darkness, but It was time for me to practice what I preach. At first, I was overwhelmed with tears, but I fully surrendered to the heavy emotion, until the anxiety and depression eventually lifted.

As my health improved so did my confidence. I came to spend some time back in my home town of Huddersfield and catch up with old friends and family members. It is November 2018 as I finish writing this introduction, and four months have passed since I arrived back in the UK. I am communicating with my daughter on a regular basis, and I am due to fly back to Sweden to spend Christmas and the new year with her.

I am uncertain what the future holds, but I know that my life experiences up until this point have shaped and prepared me to share my truth with the world. What is my truth? My truth is to help you let go of your painful past, so you can discover your truth.

Whether we realise it or not we are all going through a transformation, and many of us will resist it. The biggest lesson I have learned up until this point is that we cannot be truly happy until we are being true to ourselves, and if you are not honoring and following your truth, one way or another, life will let you know. This may mean having to make decisions that go against everything society expects you to be and do. It may mean having to delve into the unknown without any guarantees. It may also mean having to face your deepest darkest fears.

But one thing is for sure, the moment you choose to leave your "small" and "safe" conditioned cocoon created through past experiences, is the moment you will start to blossom and see your One True Reflection.

PART

1

THE SEPARATION

"A conditioned mind is never a free mind"

~ Bruce Lee

CHILDHOOD CONDITIONING

As children, we are enlightened beings, at one with life, connected to the true essence of who we are. We have no problems expressing ourselves as pure authenticity and creativity oozes out of us into all that we do. We don't try to be somebody else; we are who we are and know how to be true to who we are. We instinctively know how to express our emotions: we laugh when we are happy and cry when we are sad. There are no filters when we are children; we show ourselves to the world with little fear or resistance. And why should we have any resistance to being ourselves? Sharing our unique authenticity is the greatest gift we can give anybody. As children we do not understand why we should not be ourselves; as yet, we have no reason not to be. Innocence means not knowing any better than to live true to whom we are and enjoy life in pretty much any situation and moment. The only thing that we seem to want to do when we are children is play, explore, and enjoy life. To play is to express ourselves without the constraints or expectations of others. We are not trying to be somebody else or trying to gain acceptance, we just want to have fun. We usually only get upset when somebody tries to stop us having fun or make us do things we do not want to.

Having fun seems to be instinctive to children. This is because children are naturally gifted magicians and can create anything out of everything. They can make a castle out of a cardboard box, a dragon out of a stick, and a wonderful fairy-tale adventure out of a few old clothes.

The reason that children can have fun with little or no effort is because they are not yet carrying the heavy burden of conditioning that prevents them from being who they are. Without the same level of conditioning that us adults have, they are less distracted and more able to naturally live in the present moment. They do not dwell on the past or worry about the future, as they are connected to the only thing that is real: what is going on right now, in this very moment. How often do you see a child playing, then stop and worry about what they are going to do tomorrow, or start dwelling on what happened yesterday? When a child is playing they are totally tuned into what they are doing, and nothing else matters. When we are here in the now why would we need to think about being anywhere else, or being anybody else?

As children, we are filled with excitement and joy because we are being ourselves. It is that simple. We are aligned with who we are. So, what happens to us? Where do all our insecurities, fears and limitations come from? And why do we choose to suppress our light, or only show it on rare occasions? Why does all this natural playfulness disappear? And where does it go, leaving us adults spending the rest of our lives deep in search for a glimpse of what we once had? The truth is that our natural ability to have fun with little or no effort, and to be our true authentic selves is not lost, but just forgotten. And as we grow into adults we forget how to fully be ourselves, through the influence of the environment we are living in. It's a process that goes on throughout our childhood and, if unobserved, can carry on throughout the rest of our lives, taking us away from our natural connection with ourselves and life. We are all conditioned and pulled away from ourselves and made to believe that we are, or should be, somebody else.

It is the conditioning that we are subjected to that makes us think and behave in new ways that contradict the true self. We are taught how to be and how to act, and slowly, over the years, life becomes that very thing – an act. We emerge into adulthood, acting and pretending to be somebody we are not.

Our conditioning comes from the people we rely on to teach us about the world. They give us information, which is not necessarily true, based on their own conditioning and perspective. They may be our parents, extended family, neighbours and friends, our school teachers, or our religious teachers. Anybody that we see as an authority figure will have a greater ability to influence us and play their part in our conditioning. The 'grown-ups' will do their best to instill their conditioning into us, even if that conditioning has not helped them live a happy and successful life. We are also conditioned to prepare us for the future. But nobody can predict what will happen in the future, let alone our individual future. So, is this conditioning useful or useless? The motive behind most of our childhood conditioning is to help us live happy lives, but much of it turns into the cause of our unhappiness. This is because our conditioning takes us away from who we really are.

We are not always conditioned by what others tell us. We also create our own conditioning when we experience new and perhaps confusing situations. For example, if mum or dad leaves home, we may feel abandoned and rejected, and as we ponder on why our parent left, we may decide it is somehow our fault and believe we do not deserve love or attention.

Children lack the wisdom, maturity, and the mental capacity to understand why things are happening the way they are. This then affects their ability to create accurate understandings of the situations they are experiencing.

Sue came to me with confidence issues. She was extremely reserved, never wanting to express her views and opinions. In fact, she became anxious in any situation where she might have to speak or share something about herself. The problem was, her job as a lawyer required her to speak and be sociable, and her shyness was stopping her being successful in her work. I asked Sue to tell me about the last time that she felt like she lacked confidence. She told me about a social situation with friends and several people that she had not met before. She said that there were moments during the conversation that she wanted to speak but chose not to as she felt anxiety, fear, and a feeling of shutting down.

I could see that this must be conditioned behaviour and started to dig a little deeper. I asked her to tell me about her earliest memory of feeling anxious, afraid, and shut down. Sue immediately recalled being six years old and seeing her father beating her mother, a scene she witnessed on many occasions. Understandably, Sue became emotional as she recalled the beating, and so I asked her to tell me what she was feeling. She replied, "Anxiety, fear and a feeling of contraction." This memory exposed the cause of her confidence issues. Sue witnessed her father beating her mother on many occasions and feared that she would be beaten. Sue's mother never tried to stand up for herself and say something out of a fear of being beaten even more. Sue's subconscious created the fear and anxiety that she was always experiencing to protect her from being beaten. Her past had not been resolved and was still playing out in her life some 30 years later. Even though in adulthood there was no threat of her being beaten, the subconscious saw any situation that involved her expressing herself as threatening.

Sue's conditioning was stopping her expressing herself in situations where she consciously wanted to be more sociable. Throughout her life, Sue had allowed this fear to control and dictate the way that she communicated with others. Her father was no longer beating her mother, and Sue was now living thousands of miles away from her father, so why was she still so afraid of expressing herself? How could this fear still exist when there was no longer any threat? Our past experiences shape our present behaviours, and if we allow our conditioning to dictate our behaviours, we will forever be confined to our past.

As children, we believe what those who we love and trust tell us. Our parents are our first point of contact, and most of our conditioning comes through our interactions with them. Our parents are like gods. They are our bridge to the world we are learning to live in. We look to them to teach and show us how to behave in this world, and much of this is done through observation and mimicry. We often end up replicating their mannerisms and outlook on the world, and we can literally become our parents. As men, we tend to become our father and marry our mother, and as women we tend to become our mother and marry our father. So, if we witness our parents acting from insecurity and fear, chances are that we will adopt the same insecurities and fears they carried.

Conditioning does not start with our parents conditioning us, as they were conditioned by their parents, and so on back through the family tree. We may have conditioned traits that have been passed down through the family for hundreds of years. This explains why somebody in our family may say, “You sounded just like your grandfather then”. Chances are that we are all carrying conditioned traits that our great grandparents carried, and that those traits created the same challenges for them as they do for us today.

Our parents do the best they can with the tools that were passed down to them by their parents. But many are not yet aware how much damage can be caused by repeatedly telling children things that are not true. They do not realise they are passing down beliefs, fears and behaviours that have been in the family for generations. So, if you are unable to let go of a specific limiting fear, belief, or behaviour, it will be passed down to your children for them to try and fix.

Our conditioning is partly created through how others expect us to be. We hear admonishments like, 'Stop dreaming!', 'You can't do that!', 'You're not good enough', and, 'Grow up'. Grow up? What does that even mean? How can anybody other than you know how you should be? Are we being conditioned to believe that by 'growing up' we cannot play and have fun like we did when we were children? We never lose our ability to create magic and have fun, but as we become conditioned we forget how to. We are still capable of creating magic out of any moment, just like children do. We can act foolish, do something spontaneous, and just laugh for no reason other than life is so amazingly hilarious.

Part of our conditioning makes us believe that when we grow up and mature that childhood is over. This is partly true, but we do not have to stop having fun, playing, and enjoying life. We are all still entitled to live life with joy and excitement, yet we seldom seem to remember this. Our conditioning then begins to change our perspective of where fun comes from.

When I was traveling through South East Asia I spent some time in Cambodia. The temperature was high as I drank the last of my bottled water and put the empty bottle in the bin. Suddenly a group of children ran out of nowhere, plucked the empty bottle out of the bin and ran off towards a nearby river. They tied some string on the bottle and threw it into the river to fill it with water. They all passed the bottle to one another to have a go at a game they seemed to have invented on the spot. The fun that these children were having with an empty plastic bottle and piece of string, despite the poverty portrayed by their bare feet and rags, highlighted how much more they had on the inside than was visible on the outside. They needed very little to feel happy in that moment.

Some of the people that I met whilst traveling through Asia had very little but were the happiest people I had ever met. But how can this be? How can the people that seem to have the least seem to be the happiest? This is because they live in more remote locations that hide them from the same level of conditioning that we in the West are subjected to. That conditioning tells us that we need more of this or that to have fun or be happy, that we're not wealthy enough or we're too old, or too tired. This clever marketing has been used to make us believe that in order to feel happy, accepted or 'good enough' we must have more things. The more things, money, or perfect conditions we think we need in order to be happy and ourselves, the further away from ourselves and happiness we are taken. Children do not need things to be happy so why do we? Maybe children who have been conditioned into a world that makes them believe that they need the latest computer console or toy will believe that they need things to be happy. But if you leave a child to their own devices, with no distortion of where happiness comes from, they will express it with ease.

Children are perfect examples of how we adults would like to be. In many regards, they are our teachers. We may be filled with intelligence and an ability to use logic in situations where children maybe cannot, but when we look to the root of what everybody is searching for, we find the desire for more happiness. It's quite comical how adults are searching for what children naturally possess and express, only for us to pull them out of that state and try to educate them into a new way of living and being that even we struggle with. When we are children, we are pulled out of a world that works and gives us everything that we need, into a world that is filled with confusion and suffering, only to try as adults to step back into the world we started in. Obviously, parents have an important role in teaching children right from wrong, how to speak and most importantly, to give them love and attention. But when it comes to happiness, children know better than their parents how to achieve it, because they are it. Adults would pay a lot of money in return for a fraction of the happiness and love that naturally flows through a child.

THE SUBCONSCIOUS

Children are a clean slate. This means that all they have to offer to the world is themselves. They then begin to see the world in the same way their parents and great grandparents do.

It is through our conditioning that we start to present a different person to the world, and this is what changes our perception of the world. The foundation of our conditioning is built on core beliefs and unresolved emotions. All our core beliefs are created when we are children. Have you ever felt like you are not good enough? Well, guess what, that is a belief. Have you ever procrastinated over doing something that you enjoy? Well, that shows that you have a belief that something negative may happen if you do that thing. Our conditioning creates many limiting beliefs that can hide unseen, yet control all that we do and don't do. Imagine the subconscious as a large computer that stores all information for its user. We operate from our subconscious 95% of the time, which means that when we are operating from our subconscious, we are not actually being our true authentic self but rather, we are acting out our past and projecting our conditioning into, the present.

Our conditioning is at its most potent during our first seven years. During this time, we are operating primarily in a Theta brainwave state. The Theta brainwave is the twilight state that we find ourselves in just before we fall asleep at night, and when we have just awoken in the morning. Anything that happens, anything we are told or conclusions we come to goes straight into storage in our subconscious mind. Theta is also the hypnotic state that hypnotists put people into in order to access the subconscious mind and make relevant changes to help their clients lose weight, stop smoking or anything else they would like to change.

Children operate primarily within this brainwave state, soaking up their environment and storing events, situations, and experiences straight into their subconscious mind. The first seven years of our life is like we have our own record button switched on and we are recording everything that happens to us. The subconscious mind stores what it thinks is useful information and is designed to keep us alive and safe. It collects any data that it thinks it pivotal for our growth and protection.

Unfortunately, the subconscious makes sweeping generalizations from challenging situations that we experience and creates beliefs as a result. All these beliefs sit comfortably within our subconscious, dictating and influencing our behaviours and actions. Because we spend 95% of our time operating from our subconscious, it is very easy to end up living an unconscious and self-destructive life, depending on the type of beliefs that we are aligned with and operating from. The subconscious is like having another person standing behind you, telling what you to do 95% of the time. We are unaware when this is happening. To not be aware of our behaviour and actions until we have done something we regret is not the most ideal way to see the conditioned aspects of ourselves. But at times this is our only way to see how our conditioning is making our decisions for us.

Dr Bruce Lipton, a renowned cell biologist, has studied for many years the subconscious and our behaviours in reflection to our environment. He explains in one of his articles: “Since the subconscious programs operate outside the range of consciousness, we don’t experience ourselves playing out these behaviours. Therefore, we don’t even see ourselves sabotaging our own lives, and as a result, we don’t take responsibility for the lives we lead. We see ourselves as victims of forces outside of our control. It’s hard to own what we’ve done our whole lives. So, we perceive ourselves as victims.” We adopt an attitude of victimhood as we act unconsciously, create situations, and then become confused and saddened by the result of our actions. Without us realising, our past can be controlling everything we do and don't do.

LAYERS OF THE ONION

Through our conditioning, we develop layers, like layers of an onion. These layers are made up of the pain from past experiences, and the beliefs and ideas we have about who we are and the world. One layer is placed upon us, then another, and another. The more layers we have, the further away from our truth we are taken. The best way to know how deep your layers run is to become aware of how you feel day to day. Do you find yourself becoming angry or irritated on a regular basis? Do you feel sad or anxious and fearful for no reason?

Some people seem to become angry over seemingly insignificant things, whilst others not so much. Why is this? It is because some people have more layers than others. Somebody with many layers of anger may become angry very easily, whilst somebody else may have many layers of sadness and spend most of their life sad and depressed. But one thing is for sure, carrying all these layers around with us wherever we go can become unbearable. Just like having to wear all our clothes on a hot day.

So, why do we find ourselves carrying around our past, unable to let it go? Society has become emotionally uneducated and this means we do not know how to allow our emotions to be processed naturally. When we experience a traumatic situation, we do not have the guidance to show us how to allow the trauma to leave our system as it needs to. Unresolved emotions and trauma play havoc with the way we feel, as it bubbles away beneath the surface.

A wild animal knows instinctively how to allow trauma to leave so that it can go back to its natural state of being. I watched a video of a polar bear that was being chased by a group of people in a helicopter. They were chasing it so that they could tag it. They got as close as they could and fired their rifle to sedate and then tag it. As it lay sedated on the ice, its whole body started to shake. It looked like it was having a seizure, but in fact, the polar bear was allowing the trauma created when it was being chased, to leave. Sure enough, as soon as it regained consciousness, the bear walked away as though nothing had happened.

When we are unable to allow our emotions to be processed, they are pushed down and suppressed. Trauma is created when we experience a situation that we cannot run away from or fight against. This creates a freeze like effect. We freeze in that moment and it creates trauma. This explains why many people cannot seem to settle and find peace in their lives. Even if you live in the most tranquil and peaceful of settings you may still experience stress and panic. Why? Because you have unresolved trauma that have not been healed, and so the body believes that it is living in a dangerous environment, even if it is not. We can develop many fears and distorted beliefs about ourselves and the world because of the trauma that is trapped within. The backlog of emotional pain that we experience builds up over time, and if this is not dealt with and removed, we will never know what it feels like to be at peace. We may have glimpses of our true nature, just to remind us of what is still waiting to be remembered beneath all our layers. But these moments will be fleeting, and our layers will quickly pull us back.

The layers of conditioning that we carry block our inner light. These layers then create the separation from the truth of who we are. It is important that we clear out this backlog of past pain to allow the light of who we are to shine through and be remembered. But we must also make sure that we do not add more layers to the ones we already have. It is important that we do not create more distorted ideas about ourselves and the world. This can happen through our social conditioning.

SOCIAL CONDITIONING

The core of our conditioning is created when we are children, but it does not stop there. We continue to be conditioned by the environment we are living in. It is one thing to be able to let go of the conditioning from our past, but the challenge is not to allow ourselves to be socially conditioned in the present. The way we dress, talk, and communicate can all be influenced by the environment we live in. The history of fashion shows us how people feel a need to fit in with the crowd by dressing the same as them. This need can also be seen in the type of music we listen to, the football teams we support and religions we choose. There are many ways in which we are socially conditioned and influenced by what the majority is doing.

We often choose to live a life based more on how society expects us to be, rather than how we want to be. The word 'should' mostly comes from our conditioning. We can be doing something that we want to do but feel as though we 'should' be doing something different. This is because our conditioned behaviours are mostly fear based and will push us to conform and act the same as others. To conform means to act in accordance with what everybody else is doing, even if that is not what we want to do. Social conditioning then becomes the blueprint that we are made to believe we must adhere to. But why do so many of us choose to conform and do what we may not want to do? Is it just because society is doing it?

We chose to conform to what others are doing and what society expects from us in order to feel accepted. This comes from one of the greatest fears on the planet, the fear of rejection. Our need for acceptance has grown so strong that we will do anything to feel it. Even if that means we gain this acceptance through presenting a different person to the world. This is the person that we believe people will like and accept. We adopt a new personality and mould it around how we think others want us to be, or what others will accept. But this kind of behaviour is shrouded with fear. Choosing to live our lives out of a need for acceptance will only ever lead to further unhappiness and suffering. This fear-based need for acceptance makes us believe that as long as we conform and act in the ways that others expect us to act, do what everybody else is doing, and basically forget any sense of who we are, then we are actually being accepted. We then fulfil our need for acceptance by being somebody else and believe, that people will reject us if they see who we really are. This need for acceptance highlights the fact that we are not at one with ourselves. When we are being ourselves we feel free of any needs, especially the need to be accepted. Children are themselves and do not shrink away from others and demand to be accepted. It is our conditioning that acts like a wedge and separates us from our truth. We then find ourselves being somebody else and feeling afraid and needing validation from others. Being somebody else and chasing validation and acceptance will only keep us separate from the source of true happiness.

What do you believe will hurt more, to pretend to be somebody else for the rest of your life to satisfy your need for acceptance? Or to be yourself and do what you want with your life? This may create an obvious answer: "Well, of course it hurts more to choose to be somebody else". As obvious as this is, why are so many of us choosing to take the path that always leads to further pain and suffering? We fear the ridicule that may come through choosing to be ourselves, and different from our environment. But being different is a sign that you are choosing not to conform. To be called different or maybe even weird may be seen as a negative, when in fact, it is one of the best compliments anybody can give you. So, if anybody says, 'You're weird,' you can reply, 'Thanks!'

Our fear of rejection and need for acceptance is what makes our need to conform so strong. But we can never truly be accepted until we are able to truly accept and be ourselves. And the interesting thing is, that when we fully accept ourselves and drop our need for acceptance, we receive it in its purest form. Living our lives out of a need for acceptance makes us a slave to what we believe other people want from us. We become the person we think other people want us to be to feel accepted by them, but we then neglect who we are. And what an exhausting job it is to try and always please others to gain approval. Do you think that it is even possible to always please others?

We neglect the qualities that we possessed as children because we fear what others may think. Unconditioned children are naturally happy because they express how they feel. They are conditioned to believe it is wrong to feel and express certain emotions like sadness and anger, they shut the emotions away, and, in the process, they shut themselves away. Children say what they want to say until we teach them it is wrong, through our own inability to do the same. When we notice that somebody is harbouring an emotion like sadness, our way of communicating with them is to ask, 'What's wrong?' This very question implies there is something wrong, and that they should not be feeling that way.

We judge others for having the courage to show how they are feeling rather than keeping it suppressed and hidden. We are taught that it is good to feel good, and bad to feel bad. What if it was good to feel good, and good to feel 'bad'? This does not mean that we deliberately choose to feel bad and say that it is good to do so. No, it means that we choose to allow all emotions to be as they are, with no labels or judgments.

Allowing ourselves to feel what has not been processed is vital in our transformation. Would we then use the words 'What's wrong?', if we knew that allowing our emotions to be felt was a necessary step towards being truly happy? Maybe we would be more accepting, accommodating, and supportive of what another person is feeling. Instead of saying 'What's wrong?', we could say something like, 'It's completely OK to feel how you feel right now'. This creates a safe space, a feeling of acceptance and openness to what is being felt. We could also choose to say nothing at all, and just be available for the other person if they want to express how they feel.

When we have a judgmental approach towards emotions, we are teaching the new generation of children how not to be themselves. I look forward to when we can openly communicate how we feel with each other without the fear of judgment.

Imagine bumping into a friend whilst out shopping and they say to you, "Hey, how are you?" and you reply, "Oh, my dog just died, which triggered a great deal of sadness that is stlll passing though me. And my partner and I are working through some jealousy, thanks for asking, how are you?'. You can imagine that they may be quite shocked that you have told them exactly how you are in that moment. This shows how communication has turned into a way to say what we know other people want to hear to avoid any kind of judgement. So, when people ask how you are, most of the time they do not actually want your true answer, or to really know how you are at all. What they want to hear is something that will enable them to feel comfortable engaging in a conversation with you.

Our conditioning has turned us into very judgmental and critical people, who seem to forget that we too have our own conditioned insecurities, that need to be dealt with. We say what we think people want us to say, to keep the way we socially interact within the realms of what society expects. But these kinds of conversations are always surface level and we know deep down that we want something more, something with meaning and passion. The mundane surface level chatter is upheld by those who are not being themselves and are operating through fear. We are afraid to go deeper into conversations because of what might be revealed. This fear is two-fold, as we fear feeling what may arise from deep within, and we also fear what others may think when they see it. This is why open and honest communication can, in itself, be extremely healing. Communicating openly and honestly about how we feel, makes space for what we feel to rise up and leave. This kind of communication can also give rise to fear and resistance, which is understandable, if we have always communicated in a way that is designed to keep what we do not want to feel hidden. It feels refreshing to say how you feel with conviction. You feel a sense of freedom when you can say what you really want to say, and in the process, start moving back to who you are. When we communicate through fear and keep what we want to say hidden, we keep ourselves hidden too.

WHY?

As children, we question everything out of pure curiosity. We want to know how the world works so we ask a lot of questions. We ask questions and when we receive the answers we question the answer. “Why, Daddy? Why, Mummy?” We are intuitively using the word ‘why’ as a tool to filter out what feels right and what does not. After you have asked the question ‘why’, you will receive an answer, and if that answer does not resonate with you then maybe it is untrue, or not for you, or not the right time for you to receive it.

If the information does resonate and feel true, you will know that it is for you, and you can choose to believe it. If the information is helping to guide you back to your truth, then it is helpful. It is important for us to keep questioning what we are being told. We are vibrational beings and the energy behind information that we are being presented with is also a vibration. If we do not resonate with the information, then we know. Resonance is an indication of truth. When we resonate with what people are sharing with us, it shows that on a deep level, we are being reminded of something that we already know. So, to resonate means there is a vibrational match.

It seems that from an early age we want to make sure we are receiving correct information through our natural inquisitiveness. As we grow, we seldom ask the same kind of questions; why is this? Are we conditioned to look in a completely different direction? Are we being moulded into a system that has been created to stop our natural inquisitiveness? Once we are conditioned away from our truth, we seem to take what we are told by authority figures as gospel. This shows that the relationship that we had with our intuition as children has dramatically changed. We do not have to take everything as truth, even if that comes from so-called authority figures. Those who choose to question and challenge what they are being told when it does not feel right, are those that will think with their own mind and not the mind of another.

Even if the people offering the information are apparent authority figures, always trust your intuition and resonance with the information that is being offered to you. By not questioning and even sometimes challenging the information that we are receiving, we are inviting the risk of adding to our existing conditioning. This can turn into a never-ending cycle of deconditioning and clearing out the clutter, only to recondition ourselves with the similar clutter. We will never truly move forward and be able to reveal who we are, if we always relate to information that is not congruent with our true nature. We all have a choice; to either receive or reject the information that we are being presented with. If we do not question what we are being told when it does not resonate, we are allowing ourselves to be conditioned and even manipulated. The only way that we can let go of what does not serve us, is to follow our inner guidance. And what is right for me may not be right for you.

I feel that at some point we must go out into the world and use our intuition and self-guidance to find our way, rather than always relying on the information we are receiving from others. Just like when we learn how to ride a bike, we will use stabilizers in the beginning to help with the balance. Eventually we need to let go of this assistance and ride alone. This is the same with any information that we absorb from any teaching or organization. At what point are we going to implement and live this information to see if it works for us? We may absorb new information to try and take us away from the old. But it is important not to have new information that just adds to the old and takes us further away from who we are. Information and conditioning has turned into a way to enhance who we are. But is this even possible? How can we enhance or improve the limitless nature of who we are at our core?

We are conditioned out of our true state and the layers of our conditioning eventually turn into a separate self. We identify with this separate self and begin to see the build-up of our conditioned layers as who we are. This is when the separation from who we truly are becomes much wider and more difficult to close. But the good news is that once you realise who you are not, you are guided back to who you always have been.

PART

2

WHO DO YOU THINK YOU ARE?

“Most people are other people. Their thoughts are someone else’s opinions, their lives a mimicry, their passions a quotation.”

~ Oscar Wilde

IDENTIFICATION WITH LIMITATION

In places where elephants are kept in close quarters, such as the circus, their keepers train them by chaining them to a solid steel post set into the ground. The elephant tries to walk freely until the shackle around one leg tightens and it cannot move any further. It may pull and strain against the post, but the steel does not budge. From a young age, these elephants repeatedly experience being able to walk a few paces in any direction before being brought up short. As the elephant calf grows into a full-sized powerful creature, it comes to believe that it is impossible to move any further than the steel post allows. Once it no longer tries to pull the post out, the trainer replaces the steel post with a wooden post or stick. By this time, the elephant has the power to push over a car or pull down a house, but it makes no effort to break free. The elephant does not even think about trying. Its conditioning has won, and it lives in a world that it believes is limited by a post in the ground.

It may sadden or shock you that such an intelligent and powerful creature can be conditioned to believe that it is limited by a stick in the ground. But we humans are not so different. We are also conditioned, and grow to believe our conditioning, and deny ourselves what we are truly capable of. It is through our identification with our limiting conditioning that we also imprison ourselves within mind-made limitations.

Identification with our conditioning acts like glue and keeps us stuck in all our perceived limitations. We will never experience freedom whilst we are identified with our conditioning, as we are choosing to believe all the limiting lies that it tells us. Believing that which we are not and allowing our conditioning to limit us, keeps us forever stuck within the need to improve our lives. To believe that we are our conditioning means that we believe we are our past experiences. This means that we carry our past around with us everywhere we go and project it into everything that we do. This creates unnecessary situations and obstacles for us. In fact, the only obstacle that gets in our way, is ourselves, when we believe what our fears and insecurities say about us. Our fears and insecurities are just aspects of our conditioning, but most of us cannot discern between our conditioning and who we really are. We are not taught to tell the difference, and so our self-doubt restricts us.

So, who do you think you are? Do you think that you are too much or too little of this or that? Or maybe your past has been such a struggle that you believe that you are destined to walk the same path for the rest of your life. How do you talk about yourself, and what do you believe about yourself? We all have labels for whom we think we are, but most of them are not true. Not only are the labels that we place on ourselves not true, but the self that we have been placing them on, is not true either. Our conditioning creates a separate self, with whom most of us have identified with as our true self, and in the process, we have also forgotten who we really are. Our conditioning is just conditioning, nothing more. It is not who we are, but it seems that the majority of the population now believe that they are who they are not. Some may refer to this self as the ego. The definition of the ego is 'a sense of self'. This means that our ego is only a sense of who we are, and not who or what we truly are.

We limit our lives by believing we are who we have been conditioned to think we are. We are unknowingly choosing to believe that we are our conditioning over our truth. Being conditioned out of the connection that we have with our truth when we are children means that we have created a separate identity. I see the 'self' that we have been lead to believe we are as the conditioned self. When we focus all our attention on this fictitious self, believing it is who we are, we forget who we really are. This consistent identification with a self that is not real, severely limits our limitless potential. Identifying with the conditioned self can make us say the strangest things, like "I am angry."" I am sad." "I am too sensitive." "I am not good enough."

These "I am'" statements re-enforce our identification with our conditioning, and the longer we continue to identify with our conditioned limitations, the more we become them. One of the ways that we can stop identifying with who we are not, is by changing the way we talk about ourselves. This loosens the grip that our conditioning has over us. Instead of stating that we are what we're experiencing, we can use a more transitory way of describing our inner state. "I'm experiencing anger." "I feel sadness flowing through my body." "I have a feeling that I am not good enough." Such statements carry much less attachment and identification to what we are experiencing. Words carry a lot of power, especially when we are directing them at ourselves. Instead of saying that you are what you are experiencing and taking ownership, you stay detached and bring a level of curiosity into what is happening. This allows you to be more aware of what is happening through you rather than always thinking it is happening to you. Using a different language gives more power to your truth and less power to the lie. This makes the grip of the conditioned self-harder to take hold, just like trying to grab a wet and slippery bar of soap. Using a more positive language creates a more positive state of being and starts moving our identification away from the conditioned self, back to who we truly are.

The reason most of us believe this fictitious self is who we are, is because we need to identify with something. To not know who we are seems a scary thought, so we clutch hold of something that we can identify with as the self. Unfortunately, we choose to identify with the conditioned version of who we are, and with that comes all the doubts, insecurities, and limitations. The problem with identifying with the conditioned self is that it will have us scour the planet in search of a way to fix or improve itself. We then believe that there is something wrong with us. The only thing that is wrong is the belief that there is something wrong. We tend to compare ourselves to others whilst acting through the conditioned self. "She is better than me at that." "I would never be able to do what he does." "I am better than you." It is the conditioned self that is responsible for all our pain and suffering as it picks faults with itself.

The conditioned self is like having an extremely negative twin brother or sister that follows you around everywhere you go. Your twin will want to react to everything that happens based on past experiences. It will try to make you act in the same way it does by saying what it thinks about you and the situations you are experiencing. Your twin will also criticise you and tell you all the things you can and cannot do. You can literally split yourself into two people and see yourself as having another self that, until now, has limited you in many areas of your life. But your twin is not to be seen as the enemy, as it is understandably created through the barrage of conditioning that we are all subjected to. Just like a robot is programmed to think and act in a certain way, so are we. When I share the twin analogy with people, some of them say that their twin is more like a demon or a dark cloud that takes them over and makes them do things that they do not want to do. They explain that they lose all control and act in ways that seem foreign and out of character, just like having an argument and shouting abuse at another person only to settle down and realise what you have said. "I'm so sorry, I don't know what came over me, I wasn't being myself." I'm sure we have all had experiences like this, and the truth is that we are not ourselves when we are taken over by the conditioned self. This does not mean that we can use this as an excuse, so that after every argument we say, "I did not do anything! It was my twin!" We must take full responsibility for our actions, even if we are unconsciously hurling abuse at somebody, we must bring awareness into what has happened once the dust has settled.

Not being aware of the conditioned self means that it can take us over and act through us when the right opportunity arises. In a second, we can be filled with anger, hate, jealousy or sadness. What better bait can the conditioned self use to keep you identified with it than the unresolved pain from your past? It will use your past against you so that it can take you over and stay alive and active in the process. The conditioned self's primary objective is to survive, and it will do anything it can to stay alive. The only way that it can survive is to have you believe that it is you and you are it. This then creates a connection that acts as a power cord that feeds it energy. The longer we are identified with the conditioned self, the more power it gains and the less energy we have for ourselves – just like when you connect jump leads to another car to get the engine going again, and in the process watch your own car's energy be drained as the headlights dim. The conditioned self clearly has to get its energy from somewhere, in order to stay alive, and that place is you. To think that we have two selves may sound outrageous, but this is not a new idea. Many ancient teachings, philosophers and religions have been sharing this idea for thousands of years. One such teaching comes from the Toltec civilization from central Mexico, which flourished between the 10th and mid-12th centuries CE, and continued the heritage left to them by the earlier civilizations of the Olmec, Teotihuacano, Maya and others. The Toltecs would later pass on that heritage to civilizations such as the Aztecs, who regarded the Toltecs as a great and prosperous civilization.

Don Miguel Ruiz, the writer of such books like *The Four Agreements* and *The Mastery of Love* is a teacher of the esoteric Toltec knowledge, and refers to our conditioning as a parasite. He explains that when the parasite has taken over, we become judgmental and essentially act out of accordance with who we are, and in the process literally become somebody else. When being controlled by the parasite, the Toltecs say that we are asleep and that we no longer have free will. There are many different interpretations of the conditioned self. Maybe you already have your own interpretation of the self that tries to get you to act in ways that are out of alignment with who you are. The conditioned self has many faces: it can be jealous, paranoid, anxious, fearful, stressed, and angry.

The conditioned self can only become active when we are acting unconsciously. At any given moment, we are either being ourselves or being somebody else. We are either acting through truth or our conditioning. We are either conscious or unconscious. Who we choose to be, can feel like a stranger at times. You are not your emotions, beliefs, or conditioning. You are what is hidden beneath them all. Beyond the lie of who we are, is the truth of who we are. To access this truth, we must first realise the lie that most of have been living. This means seeing the conditioned self for what it really is: an illusionary sense of self. The truth is that we are not our conditioning and therefore we are not the conditioned self. So, the conditioned self is not a 'self' at all. However, to be able to create a discernment and for the purposes of this book, I will be referring to us as having two selves: the true self and the conditioned self.

The conditioning that we endure through our experiences can knock us out of alignment with the truth. This then changes the limitless personality that we have as children into a limited persona. We start to believe that we are the limitations that were created through past conditions. To be conditioned is one thing, but to identify with our conditioning and believe it is who we are, is another. The problem is most of us believe that we are our conditioning. So much so, that we severely limit ourselves.

It can seem quite outrageous to believe that for most our lives we have been identifying with who we are not. Just like us wearing a costume and believing that we are the person that we have dressed up as. Imagine, for a second, that last Saturday you went to a fancy-dress party dressed as Superman and spent the evening pretending to fly with one arm stretched out in front. Then, when you went to work on Monday, you were still wearing your underpants over the woolly tights and telling everyone you really were Superman. Sounds crazy, right? We are doing the same through our identification with our conditioning. Our conditioning is our costume. We can see it just as that, a costume, a false identification, or we can choose to keep wearing the red cape, believing that we are something that we are not, and wondering why we don't leave the ground when we try to fly. It would not be such a bad thing if we all believed that we were Superman, who is strong and wants to help others through his love for humanity. But the truth is that most of our conditioning is limiting and gives us the opposite of the characteristics that Superman has. It turns us into Clark Kent, Superman's nervous, clumsy, stuttering, newspaper reporter alter ego, created to hide his superhero abilities and allow him to go about his daily business in the human world.

We also have a costume of conditioning that we use to go about our daily business. Unlike Superman, we believe it and seem to have lost our connection with who we are in favour of our limited conditioned costume.

Learning the difference between the conditioned self and the true self, brings more control and freedom into your life. You can begin to clearly distinguish between the self that wants to express itself, and the self that wants to stay in one spot, stagnate and wear a mask of insecurity. The fearful, insecure self, whose behaviour brings nothing but pain is just a distraction from our truth. Beneath all our insecure conditioned layers is the self that wants to go play, explore, and shine.

One of the key ways that this fictitious self keeps its hold over us is through our incessant stream of thinking. We are bombarded with different thoughts and told all the things we should and should not do. We then identify with this inner voice and believe that we are what the thoughts say about us.

THE INNER VOICE

The conditioned self creates mental chatter that we do not know how to switch off. The more that we identify with this mental chatter and believe what it says, the tighter its grip becomes. The voice that we have in our head, which tells us what we should and should not do, is also part of the conditioned self. We can either believe what this voice says, or we can see it for what it really is. Those who choose not to listen to the limiting internal chatter are the ones who can transcend their perceived limitations and move closer to the truth of who they are. Thoughts are just thoughts, nothing more, but we are drawn towards them, and believe them. Unfortunately, most of us are lost in our negative limiting chatter, which not only disempowers us but prevents us from being truly ourselves.

Our programmed upbringing teaches us to spend most the time in our heads, trying to understand the world and ourselves. The conditioned mind becomes the greatest distraction of all, as it tells us what it thinks life is and what we should do. Life then becomes a mixture of concepts and labels. At our core, there is nothing to be figured out or understood. We are the solution trying to solve itself. Once we begin to understand who we are not, we can start to remember who we are and always have been.

Believing what our conditioning says, makes it extremely difficult to see the wood for the trees. At times, we can feel as though there is a war raging inside us, between the voice saying what we should do and our hearts telling us to do the opposite. This is a clear indication that we have created a separate conditioned identity. This battle can go on for years, until something has to give, and often in our 40s, many of us go through what is termed a 'mid-life crisis'. Midlife crisis is a term first coined by Elliott Jacques, and refers to a critical phase in human development, based on the change of character, or periods of transition. A mid-life crisis is experienced by some people as they realise they have reached a midpoint in their lifespan. They can experience conflicts or dissatisfaction within themselves because of unrealised goals, self-perceptions, or physical changes as a result of ageing or health issues. According to psychologist and writer Oliver Robinson, "A midlife crisis is defined as a period characterized by unstable mental and emotional health, altering the course of life of those affected by it."

When experiencing a mid-life crisis, people may reassess their achievements in terms of their dreams. The result may be a desire to make significant changes in areas such as career, work/life balance, marriage, romantic relationships, finances, or physical appearance. If this crisis can alter the course of those affected by it, could that mean that it is a catalyst for change? Could this crisis be an opportunity for the conditioned self to be released and our truth to be realised? I see a midlife crisis as an emotional crisis of identity. This shows that people are unknowingly trying to find who they are, amidst all the conditioning, that has convinced them, to some degree, they are somebody else. Spending 40-odd years resisting who we truly are and pretending to be who we are not creates internal conflict and friction. Eventually it erupts into an emotional crisis of identity. "If I am not this, then who am I?" The way that we are affected by any crisis varies from person to person, but how we treat this turning point is vital for our connection back to truth.

The chatter that goes on upstairs can make us act abnormally. I'm sure we have all been in those situations where we are conversing with a group of people and something enters our head that we would like to share. Another person is still talking, so we eagerly wait our turn to disclose some information that we feel called to share. A voice then pops into your head and says, “You can’t say that, what if nobody understands what you are saying?”, “What if somebody is offended by what you are thinking of saying?”, “Even worse, what if everybody thinks you’re strange and rejects you?”. You identify with the thoughts. You begin to question whether you should share what you were going to share. Now you doubt yourself. This doubt creates a lack of confidence and maybe even fear, and so when the moment to speak finally comes, you decide not to. You have slipped into the conditioned self. Then, just before the conversation is over, somebody else says the very thing that you were going to say. Everyone is ever so impressed and show their respect towards the knowledgeable and interesting individual who shared this information. You walk home kicking yourself, wishing you had said what you wanted to say.

Sometimes our voice of reason and logic can be useful, but we must discern between whether our thoughts are there to help or hinder us. The conditioned self is fuelled by fear and will tell us anything it can to move us away from having itself exposed. This means that we limit ourselves when we trust the advice that the conditioned self-delivers to us, bowing to its every suggestion. Fears diminish when we are aligned with our truth and see the conditioned self for what it really is. Imagine a world class athlete believing their negative inner dialogue. Just before a race their conditioned self says, “You know you won’t win this race, don’t you?”, and the athlete, believing what is being said, walks back to the changing rooms, and doesn't even attempt to run the race. Most of us are identified with this voice, believing it is who we are, allowing it to hold us back from making the very first step to becoming an athlete, musician, actor, doctor, or any path that we choose to follow.

We are allowing the limiting conditioned self to steer us away from our passion and purpose. Top athletes are lucky enough to have personal trainers and coaches, who not only work with helping them develop physically, but also mentally. The mental coaching focuses on using self-belief and visualisation techniques that make the athlete believe that they have already run, and won, the race. Athletes recondition their conditioning by removing the old limiting thinking and replacing it with new limitless thinking. They are literally training their minds to think differently.

The mind has a great way of creating stories and scenarios about the future. When we allow the mind to suck us into these exaggerated movies, we begin to believe them. This can create anxiety and fear to the point that we have to create a plot to prevent these scenarios happening. We fabricate in our minds something that was likely ever going to happen, and in the process, make ourselves feel terrible. We can even become angry at people who, in our minds, we have seen treat us badly. We may even choose not to speak to this person again, because of what we imagine they have done to us. The mind can grab us and disempower us in seconds, by linking potential events to something that happened in the past, to make the story seem more believable and realistic. We can dismiss our thoughts when they try to get our attention and kidnap us, or we can believe them and be held ransom for the rest of our lives.

How did we end up spending so much time in our heads? We think, rather than feel, our way to decisions. It seems like our bodies have become the vehicle to carry around our heads. When we think our way through life, we create a disconnection from the intelligence and creativity of our bodies. Our intuition becomes dormant, and we perceive the voice in our head, which tells us what to do and what not to do, as our identity. We then trust this voice and follow its guidance. Is this because as a society we are conditioned to spend more time in our heads? I think so. The problem I see with this approach to life is that we try to understand everything on a mental level whilst dismissing our intuition, which is the part of us that always knows best.

It's quite frightening to see how lost we have become within the prison of our minds. This intense distraction from our truth is the antithetic to our potential.

It was my incessant thinking and identification with my thoughts that resulted in my long-term illness. I would be lost within my head for large proportions of the day. I had a river of thoughts flowing through my mind, most of which were negative. I would entertain, and then believe the thoughts. My mind would then develop more exaggerated thoughts and stories. The thought of not thinking used to scare me. I used to think that if I did not think, I would lose my mind. Thinking is not the enemy, our relationship with it is, especially when our thoughts become negative and we believe those thoughts. Identifying with our thinking can be damaging because thoughts trigger feelings. If we relate to a constant flow of limiting thoughts, we begin to have a constant flow of limiting emotions. Limiting emotions create stress, and stress is the biggest killer on the planet. Identifying with your thinking means that you are allowing yourself to become unnecessarily burnt out, sick, and even seriously ill. Why is it that even though we seem to have made huge advances in our understanding of health, we still have such an epidemic of stress? It's because we are neglecting the very thing that is causing the problem, which is our identification with our thoughts. Instead of giving people tablets to suppress the symptoms, we should be looking deeper into what's causing them. Just knowing that we are not our thinking and choosing not to believe what our conditioned mind tells us, can be enough to reclaim our energy and life.

Our negative inner dialogue is not the problem, our identification with it is. I used to think that only crazy people would walk around talking to themselves, but instead of verbalising, we are allowing the mind to chatter inside. I enjoy doing a bit of people watching when I'm out and about. I notice the extent to which we have become lost within this internal chatter. I see people laugh when they are replaying a story in their heads. Or venting their frustration out loud as they recall a not so nice memory. Nothing is happening externally in that moment to make these people either happy or angry other that their mind reminding them of something that happened in the past or better yet, something they think may happen in the future. As a society we have all become a little crazy as we listen to, and believe, the voice in our heads. But what makes a crazy person crazy? Can it be that they have become totally identified with their thoughts and are verbalising what they are thinking? To go to the doctor and say, 'I hear voices' would surely have them send us for more expert 'professional' help. But we are all hearing voices with the constant narration happening over everything we do. So, does this mean, that we are all crazy?

To dis-identify with our conditioned thinking is what will save us. Our minds are then open to the truth. But let's face it, it's not easy to just decide one morning to stop thinking. And it is not about trying to stop anything, it is about knowing that the thoughts that flow through our heads do not belong to us. But we have become addicted to thinking. So much so that we are lost in thought for most the day.

ANALYSE VS REALISE

Being caught in our conditioned thinking will always result in a feeling that there is something wrong. Our thoughts are part of the conditioned self, and thinking is its greatest tool to create a distraction. If we are identified with our thinking, we are connected to the conditioned self and all that comes with it. This means that we will never escape our perceived insecurities, as they are all part of our conditioning. A thought may pop up into your head when you are preparing something to eat. You gravitate towards the thought as it is about somebody who treated you badly. Before you know it, you are lost in your thoughts, feeling angry at the person that treated you badly. This may have happened many years ago, and the person could now be dead, but through your analysation of the situation, you have been pulled into a limited state of being. You are then identified with the conditioned self and all that comes with it. Have you noticed how some thoughts can pull you in more than others? You may be peacefully enjoying life when suddenly a thought pulls you in. The reason that some thoughts can cunningly lure us back into identification with the conditioned self, is that they have a belief or unresolved emotions behind them that we feel drawn to investigate. These are the type of thoughts that can feel like they are pulling us into a black hole.

I remember when I was spending one year living on a beautiful island called Koh Phangan, in Thailand. I spent a great deal of my time there in meditation and self-reflection. This allowed my mind to become quiet and silent, and I felt at peace for the first time in my life. One morning something profound happened. I was deep in meditation and I felt something erupt from within me. It was like nothing I had ever experienced before. I felt a burst of energy from the base of my spine that seemed to come from the depths of my soul and leave the top of my head. I stood up and walked to my bathroom like a baby walking for the first time. I felt more present than ever before. I peered through the window that looked out onto the ocean. It was interesting because my window had wooden bars that made me feel as though I was in prison. I realised that I had been imprisoning myself through my identification with my thinking. I jumped on my scooter and headed into the main part of town to grab some food. I was driving back to my hut when a thought entered my mind: "How will you function if you don't think?" I contemplated this thought, and that thought lead to another thought, and ten or so minutes later I was lost in a heavy stream of thinking. My thinking was so intense that I forgot I was riding my scooter. I had to pull over and ground myself, as I was overwhelmed and lost within the thoughts that had consumed my mind. I had been sucked back into a heavy stream of thinking that completely stole my awareness. This experience showed me the drastic contrast between being present and at one with life, compared to being lost in analytical thinking.

Thinking can be addictive, as without it, who are we? I was afraid that I would just vanish or go crazy if I did not think. But what I was afraid of creating through letting go of my conditioned thinking, I was creating by holding onto it. This was not the first and only insight that I had into how my analytical thinking was keeping me trapped in my conditioned self. Not long after I had left the UK to travel the world, while I was in Vietnam, I decided to fly to Peru and spend time with a shaman drinking Ayahuasca. My identification with my thinking was more severe at this point and I was desperate for help. After doing extensive research into this powerful medicine, I left Vietnam, took five flights, and spend 35 hours travelling into the Amazon. For those who have never heard of Ayahuasca before, it is an ancient medicinal plant that has been used for thousands of years to treat almost anything from depression to cancer. It also happens to be one the world's more potent hallucinogens.

Upon arrival at the retreat, I was greeted by others who were also looking for a way out of their suffering. Some were suffering more than others. One woman had fibromyalgia and spent three years in bed with chronic pain.

The first few days I was at the retreat was focused on a short detoxification. We were all given tobacco water to drink to help purify our bodies prior to the drinking of the Ayahuasca. This allows the plant medicine to work as deeply as possible, with fewer toxins in the way diluting the experience. After drinking the tobacco water, I felt terrible for three hours, needing to vomit. After hearing the retching sound of the others who had drunk the tobacco water echoing around the retreat I finally purged, such a relief. Then came the ceremonies, which were held in a large round wooden hut called The Maloka, situated deeper into the jungle. We sat in a circle in the pitch black and waited for the Shaman to light his candle, which was the signal that it was time to step up to his altar and drink the Ayahuasca. We would take it in turns to walk over to the altar, take the wooden goblet and drink the worst tasting liquid I have ever consumed. We were then asked to go and sit or lie down and relax, to allow the drink to take effect, whilst the Shaman sang his beautiful Icaros.

In one of the ceremonies, I lost my mind and was rocking back and forth with no concept of reality. I had another experience of being possessed by a demon. One of the most interesting and amusing experiences I had was when I thought the shaman leading the ceremony had decapitated me. I was sat in the lotus position as the shaman sang his Icaros over me. I thought I saw a knife in his hand, which then made me think that he wanted to chop off my head. I closed my eyes tightly, and then I thought that he had, indeed chopped off my head. As I was slowly coming back from my experience, I called over the owner of the retreat. "John?" I said as quietly as I could, out of respect for the others who were still deep within their own experiences. "What?" he replied. "Can you please come over for a second, I have a question to ask you." In total darkness, I heard him come scrambling over on his hands and knees. "What's wrong?" he said. "Where is my head?" I asked him, my eyes still firmly closed. I heard him snigger quietly. "It's on your shoulders," he replied. I slowly opened my eyes and, with a sigh of relief, touched my head and then neck to make sure everything was still intact.

As comical as this may sound, I really did think he had chopped off my head. It was not until the next morning that I realised that the ceremony and all my other experiences were a strong message for me to get out of my head. I was being shown that I was spending so much time in my head, that the only way I would be able to stop thinking, was to have my head chopped off. The medicine has a very interesting and direct way of opening our eyes to how and why we are suffering, helping us see what we otherwise cannot. I needed the many harsh and direct lessons during my experiences to show me my conditioned self and limiting behaviour. I could clearly see who I was being and how that was affecting my life. This beautiful plant medicine was able to highlight the root of my health issues and many of the insecurities I was dealing with at the time. I had become addicted to thinking and would analyse almost everything that happened to me.

My realisation and transformation came not only through the medicine, but through an energy healer who was, at the time, working at the retreat. Paul was very intuitive and, on my arrival, had seen that I was spending a great deal of time up in my head. When I was coming close to the end of my stay at the retreat, Paul shared something with me that had a profound effect on my life and inspired this section of the book. We were talking about the changes I had made during my month at the retreat. He could see that I was becoming more aware of the behaviour that was making me ill. I told him that before I came to the retreat, I always needed to analyse situations. He told me that analyse is the same as anal-eyes. He said to analyse is to look through your arse: it's always covered in shit and distorted. He then said, "But to realise is to use your real-eyes."

Laughing to myself, I went away to my little hut in the jungle to lie on my bed and ponder over what he had just told me. I felt a shift, I knew that most of what I had experienced in my life had come through my constant need to analyse situations, out of fear. If a situation did not go exactly as I would have liked it to go, I would find myself analysing it, filtering through every comment made and every look that a person gave me. I realised that when I analysed situations, I was searching for something to worry about. Worry leads to fear, and fear disempowers and cripples us. I also realised that, not only was I stirring up unnecessary fear by thinking that I had found some truth in my analysis of a situation, but I was also giving energy and focus to something that was not true. Where focus goes, energy flows and I knew that I was not making my life any easier by creating situations and giving them so much focus and analytical attention. Once I began to let go of my need to analyse everything, I began to see the situations unfold in a completely different way.

Using our real eyes instead of looking through our anal eyes means that we are changing our perception of the world, and therefore, changing ourselves and the world. When we recollect a memory and start picking through the pieces to try and understand on a mental level why it happened, why he or she said this or that, why they left without saying goodbye, or why he did not return my call, we are looking for something to worry about. After a good round of losing ourselves in the mind, we may have something to latch onto and worry about. An analytical mind is used to find the cause of a perceived problem. But what if there was never a problem in the first place? What if we are trying to find a solution to a problem that we have created? And what if we are giving energy to something that was never actually there to begin with, and in the process, manifesting a situation that never needed to happen? We tend to go away and dwell on situations, thinking of all the things that we said during the conversation, and all the things the other person said or did not say, and all the things that they are now probably saying to everybody else.

To use our real eyes and observe a situation, creates a level of detachment from what is happening. This means that we are also emotionally detached and less likely to be pulled into a limited state of being. We can see what is happening without being affected or influenced by it. There is a vast difference between observation and analysis. When you visit an art gallery, you can choose to treat this experience in two ways. You can gaze at the paintings with awe and curiosity, have a feeling of what the painting portrays, and just appreciate it for what it is. Or you can stand and stare at the painting for hours trying to figure out what it means, analysing all the different parts of the picture, the brush strokes, without just allowing it to be seen for what it truly is; Art. We are doing the same with life as we try and analyse everything that is happening in any given moment, rather than just allowing it to be. We can then observe life just like we observe a painting and appreciate it for what it is. When we view the world through our real eyes, we see it for what it is, with no labels of good or bad, wrong, or right. This approach to life brings out a different attitude, and, in the process, a different relationship with what is happening. Being over analytical means that we are trying to figure life out through the perception of the conditioned self, but life is not meant to be figured out or even understood, it is meant to be lived.

We can become lost in all the mind-made concepts of who we think we are. The challenge for many of us, is that we do not know we are living within an illusion created by the conditioned self. This is because we are identified with the conditioned self as the true and only self. To know who you are not, creates space for you to be who you are. And once you have seen the truth beyond the illusion, you will not settle for anything else.

PART

3

LOST IN THE ILLUSION

"As a holistic being, you shatter the illusion of your separateness and reveal your connection to everything. This empowers you in a way that the ego-driven self could never contemplate."

~ Wayne Dyer

SEEING THE TRUTH

It can be challenging to see the truth when we have spent most of our lives believing a lie. Even when the truth has always been right in front of us, we choose to look the other way or believe there is no other way. The conditioned self will have us look at the world through its interpretation, which means it will do all that it can to keep us seeing a distorted version of the world and ourselves. It will have us chase endless goals in the belief that they will help us find the same level of happiness we had as children. But this is a clever ploy for us not to find what we are looking for. Just like a magician uses smoke and mirrors to distract us from seeing what is really happening, so can the conditioned self. But an illusion is an illusion; it is not true. To believe that we are something that we are not, keeps our focus on the lie when the truth is in plain sight.

The conditioned self will have us wasting time chasing our tail for the rest of our lives unless we challenge the idea we have of ourselves and the world.

I see how, as adults, we are becoming lost in the search for happiness. We can try to attain happiness through many outlets that will always be short lived. Many companies are doing very well out of the search for happiness through their marketing. However, no tangible product can ever give us the deep true form of happiness that is available to us. We are lost in the illusion, chasing the pleasures of the world, believing that they will fulfil our deep yearning for what we had as children. But what the material world has on offer can never replicate the true happiness that is already within.

The things we chase in the world are just a distraction that keep us looking outward rather than inward. After achieving or obtaining something tangible, we may feel some satisfaction, but it eventually wears off to reveal the same dissatisfaction that was driving our need to get what we wanted. Even though we know the things of the world can never truly give us the kind of happiness we are searching for, we still find ourselves chasing the next thing. The conditioned self will make us believe that we cannot be happy until this has happened, or that has happened, or we have this, or we have that. The conditioned self is never satisfied. It always needs more – more acceptance, more validation, more approval from others, and more stuff, lots more stuff. The conditioned self always wants more, and more is never enough.

The illusionary world that we live in has been greatly shaped by our need to have possessions to feel happy. It's as though we have been blinded to what is truly available by the belief that we can find ourselves in things. Our search for happiness will never be fulfilled whilst we are looking for it through what is creating our unhappiness: our conditioning.

Most of us have forgotten how to be ourselves. This is clearly down to the amount of time we have spent being somebody else. To 'find yourself' means to remember and be yourself, your true self. Surprisingly, being who we are is the easy part, the hard part is learning how to stop being who we are not. The question then, is how do we know when we are being ourselves? Simple, we feel happy. And what is happiness? I used to see happiness as a fleeting emotion that was only available when I had achieved something or purchased something new. This could not be further from the truth. We can own all the cars and flat screen TVs in the world, but eventually the novelty wears off and we need more things to feel happy again. This type of happiness is not happiness at all, but rather a synthetic version of the true happiness that is always available to us. This seems to be the kind of happiness that most of the population are chasing.

Is happiness something that happens to you? Most of us see happiness as being reliant on and limited to something coming from outside of us, that triggers within us a feeling that we have labelled as happiness. However, such a view means that our happiness is entirely subject to our external circumstances. Does this mean that we can only be happy when our circumstances match our expectations? No, happiness is not just subject to external factors, happiness is our natural state of being, it is who we are. When you drill deep into what makes you feel happy, it is not when you have everything, it is when you do not need anything. There is a difference. True happiness is the state that we are in when we feel complete, whole, and not lacking anything. This is because we do not lack anything when we are being ourselves. When you take a deeper look into what we are searching for is not more happiness, we are searching for ourselves. We are all looking to get back in touch with who we truly are. We are trying to rekindle what we had as children. To be identified with the conditioned self, we know something is not right, we feel severely depleted of happiness. This is why we all start searching for what we once had. Maybe some know, and others don't, but we all want to be happy, and cannot ever be truly happy until we are being who we truly are.

Let me ask you a question: when in your life did you feel the happiest? Feel into this question and allow your mind to take you to the memories. Was it when you bought new clothes? Was it when you went to eat in an expensive restaurant? Or maybe it was a moment when you felt complete, relaxed, and able to fully be yourself? The reason that many of us seem to be franticly trying to engineer a perfect life is for one reason: to create the right environment so that we can be ourselves again. And how do you feel when you can be yourself? Happy! We believe that if we work hard enough to one day make our life perfect, we can be ourselves and therefore be happy. Trying to find the right relationship is an attempt to feel whole again and able to be ourselves. Even the moments during sex may seem like we are enjoying the stimulation, which is a big part of love making. But when we are in a peak orgasm we lose all concept of 'self' and feel connected and whole again. Even if just for a moment, those few seconds give us a true release from a world of pain and separation, into a world of total peace and connection. We chase more money so we don't have the constant feeling of lack and scarcity hanging around our necks. When we have money, we may feel a momentary feeling of safety and security, which allows us to sink back into a state of wholeness. But this will eventually wear off. No matter how much money we have, it will never be enough to give us the pure state of wholeness we are searching for. To chase our true nature through experiences and things is never going to last. It will only give us a glimpse into what is always available.

To be lost in an illusion means we have no idea we are living in one. We become comfortable with how we see the world and believe that our version of reality is the only one that is true. Even if the world we are seeing is not making us happy, we may choose to keep seeing it that way. Plato's Allegory of the Cave is a great example of how we can live within an illusion, rather than the true reality that exists beyond it. The Greek philosopher Plato illustrated the difference between reality and illusion with a story about some men who lived all their lives in a cave. These men were chained to pillars and could see only shadows cast on the back wall of the cave by a fire that burned behind them, out of their sight. The men took great pride in their interpretive abilities – yet all the time they were looking at shadows, mere illusions. Then, one of the men broke out of his chains and made his way out of the cave, where he discovered a whole new world. When he re-entered the cave to tell his friends about his marvellous epiphany, they refused to believe him and got so angry with him they wanted to kill him. Of course, there are several important philosophical lessons to be mined from Plato's cave allegory, one being the fact that a metaphysical world exists independent of human experience and observation. Plato also intended his story to illuminate the life of his teacher, Socrates, who was killed by the Athenian government for challenging ancient Greece's view of truth and reality. Plato's story illustrates how easy it is to sleepwalk through life without questioning if it is true.

How do we break free from this illusion that we call life? The first step is to know that we are in an illusion. This can be a difficult task, as when we are acting out subconscious conditioned behaviours, we are doing so unconsciously, and this is when we are lost in the illusion. Most of the population never even think to challenge the life they are living, believing that this is the only thing available to them. But a growing number of people are becoming disillusioned with the illusion and feel on a deep level that there is more available to them. This feeling and knowing rests inside all of us. However, the longer we believe in the illusion, the harder life becomes, and the deeper into hell we are pulled.

YOUR PERSONAL HELL

The idea of hell can have a strong hold on the human imagination. Virtually every religious tradition has some version of it. In the West, even people who have never been inside a church are familiar with the traditional image of Hell as a fiery, underground abode where horned devils with pitchforks torment the damned for eternity. But does Hell really exist? I believe that Hell has been widely misperceived, especially due to the religious views and teachings.

In the book *A Course in Miracles* written and edited by Dr Helen Schucman, with portions transcribed and edited by William Thetford, there are several references to Hell. "The belief in Hell is inescapable to those who identify with the ego." This quotation says that we suffer and create our own personal hell when we are identified with the ego and the conditioned version of who we think we are. *A Course in Miracles* then makes further references to hell and the ego saying, "Hell is only what the ego has made of the present." Finally, the Course gives us good news that, "There is no Hell." Neither the afterlife version nor the earthly version of Hell is real at all. Hell is purely a figment of our tormented imagination, the projected nightmare of our own separation from the truth of who or what we are, and the identification with that which we are not. If Hell, is a state of mind, does this mean that Heaven is just a state of mind too? Helen and Bill also talk about the true definition of Heaven, claiming that it is already within us. They don't just say that the

Kingdom of Heaven is within you, they say, "The Kingdom of Heaven is you."

We can use whatever language we want to try and describe what or who we truly are, but the truth is that we are powerful beyond measure and description. We have a choice whether we live in Heaven or Hell. To live in Hell comes from our decision to keep identifying with who we are not. All the conditioning from the past is not who we are, yet we have become lost in the illusion and believe that we are our conditioning. The many years we have suffered through the belief we are our past can be stopped as soon as we realise this is not who we are. This is the way to Heaven, which is not just a state of mind, it is reality. Hell is created when we believe we are anything other than what we truly are. It is not a place that we go to when we die, it is a place that we create here on this planet.

When we are stuck within our own self-created Hell, life looks miserable and bleak. We can see only the negative aspects of other people, situations, places, and ourselves. Depression is just another way of saying that somebody is trapped within their own self created and perpetuated Hell. To be depressed is to be fully identified with who we are not. When we are lost in our identification with the conditioned self we suffer, and this creates the hellish experience that we try to break out of.

Iv'e had enough !!,
...please somebody
show me a way out
of this hell !!
EXiT
WAY OUT

The conditioned self is an illusionary state of being that relies on your engagement with it to stay alive. It is made up of conditioned thoughts and emotions that feed each other on a loop. In Buddhism, they call this trap the Wheel of Samsara. When we are caught in the Wheel of Samsara, we are identified with the conditioned self, and more specifically with our limiting thoughts and emotions. We are then lost in our limited state of being, believing it is who we are. When you believe your thoughts, you are pulled into them. You then give your energy to what is not real and keep the wheel turning.

We are all capable of leaving the Hell that we have created for ourselves. However, some of us may not want to. Our painful patterns are repeated to avoid perceived greater pain. We can become addicted to substances that are helping to suppress unresolved emotions. We can stay in the wrong relationships out of a fear of experiencing loss. We may abandon healthy relationships out of a fear of love. We develop many distorted patterns that are helping us on some level avoid unwanted pain. However, it is important that we allow any pain that is blocking our light to be allowed to leave. The painful patterns that we find ourselves caught in, are at their core, a need to avoid pain. Patterns can then become a paradox as we end up creating pain to avoid pain. Take notice when you feel the most distracted or pulled into patterns. By doing this you can start to see and feel any emotional pain that you have been avoiding.

I once worked with a woman called Zoe. Zoe and her mother had many fights and she held a great deal of resentment and anger towards her. Zoe came to our first session wearing sunglasses. I asked her to remove them so I could look at her eyes and notice any changes in her emotional state. She took them off and began telling me about times when she and her mother had had fights. I noticed a slight emotional change, so I interrupted Zoe and asked, "What are you feeling right now?" She carried on talking and talked her way out of the emotion that I saw in her eyes. She then triggered herself again with another part of the story. So, I asked again, "What are you feeling right now?" She tried to start talking again. I knew that she was distracting herself from feeling the emotion that was trapped inside. Because of this I interrupted again and said quite firmly, "Stop talking." Zoe tried to talk, I said again, "Stop talking. Look at me." Zoe stopped talking and looked at me. I softly said, "What do you feel right now?" I stayed quiet as I witnessed her eyes fill with tears and she began to cry. "I feel anger...resentment," she said. So, we began to release these emotions.

Zoe came to see me and wanted to let go of her repressed anger, which she had become skilled at distracting herself from feeling. Not only did she choose to keep her sunglasses on when I was talking to her, she also tried to keep talking her way through the emotions that were being triggered. This was her unconscious, and maybe even conscious way of avoiding what she did not want to face and feel. After several sessions with me, she confessed that she also had a drinking problem. She said that every night she would drink up to eight glasses of wine. She was unconsciously self-medicating and trying to suppress the emotions that she had suppressed. After several sessions with me, Zoe explained that she not only felt that her anger towards her mother had pretty much gone, but she also did not drink as much anymore. She said that now, after one or two glasses of wine, she felt she'd had enough.

When we are living life through the conditioned self we can play out many different patterns, all of which are designed to keep us away from ourselves. If we are busy repeating old patterns that always lead to the same unnecessary suffering, the conditioned limited self is happy. But if we are playing out our patterns through a self that is only able to operate when we are not conscious or aware, how can we ever hope to see change? Fortunately, we sometimes receive assistance that snaps us out of the illusion we are lost in. This assistance may not always come how we would like it to, but it is always exactly what we need.

LIFE'S NUDGE

There comes a point during the experience of darkness when we are jolted out of our illusions. This jolt may be a severe illness or even a near-death experience. It is a sobering moment that wakes us up, just like a heavy slap around the face, followed by a shake. Many people who have had a near-death experience go on to achieve amazing things. It seems that they are literally being snapped out of the trance they had been living in for most of their lives. This sudden shift in their perception and paradigm enables them to see the world as it is without their unconscious conditioned behaviours clouding their sight. Pain and suffering will push us further and further into a corner to help us see how our behaviours were the cause of our suffering all along. When we finally see how these patterns bring nothing but pain, we can instantly let go of them, because why would we consciously make ourselves suffer? We become comfortable doing what we have always done, whilst hoping that something will change and improve. This can make people invite something into their life to act as a catalyst for change. Some people lose everything they own and believe that something terrible has happened. But what if this so-called loss was creating space for something better to arrive?

Life is not out to hurt us or make us suffer, it wants the best for us all. Sometimes it has to be something challenging that makes us wake up and see who we have been choosing to be. This is a shock to the system that says, "What are you doing?!" When we are lost in the illusion, we become complacent and if life flows to complement our complacency, how are we ever going to objectively see who we are choosing to be? If life brings challenge after challenge, it can become demoralising, to say the least. But we often refuse to see what life is trying so hard to show us. Sometimes we need the rug to be pulled from under our feet, so we can see what we have been doing to ourselves.

When I was living in Thailand, I came down with a terrible fever, the worst I have ever experienced. When it hit, I was going out quite a bit, getting high and was neglecting the healing and therapy work I intended to do. I was so feverish, it felt like my face was melting, so I decided to go to the doctor. When the nurses took my temperature, they looked at each other and quickly rushed me into the doctor's office. The doctor diagnosed me with dengue fever. I will never forget how the doctor looked at me and said, "This is serious, you could die." He explained, "If you die, it will be on day seven, as your blood platelets will be too low, and you will bleed to death."

I was not sure what to say, so I thanked him and checked myself into the hospital. I was hooked up to a drip and had my temperature checked regularly. On my sixth day in hospital, a middle-aged man arrived, occupying the bed next to me. His family came also and were relaxing next to his bed reading magazines and casually talking with each other. The man's wife leaned over and pointed to the fan that was blowing warm air onto my face, providing a tiny bit of relief from the fever. She asked me if I could turn it off as it was bothering her husband. I explained that I had dengue fever and needed it on. She said ok and sat back down. I glanced over to her husband and watched him for a few moments. He let out a deep breath and seemed to lose consciousness. I looked at him in shock, something was wrong. His family suddenly noticed and screamed out to the nurses, who came running in like tag team wrestlers. They dived on his bed and started trying to resuscitate him. He was dying. Then in flew the doctor and he tried his best to get this man's heart working again. I remember thinking that if I had turned off the fan this might not be happening.

Eventually the nurses and the doctor stopped, and so did the man's heart. He was dead. His family knelt and prayed next his bed. The other patients would walk passed and take a little look and then carry on doing what they were doing. I lay looking at this dead man for some time until I suddenly had a slap of realisation: I had been neglecting my life. I was not doing what I had come to Thailand to do. I was getting high and wasting my time. Maybe it was fear, I was not sure, but as I sat and looked at this dead man, and his family crying, I too started to cry. Firstly, came tears of sadness for the man who had just died, and his family. Then tears of frustration at myself, and then tears of determination. I felt blessed to have seen this man pass away right in front of my eyes.

Death reminded me of life. The contrast was so extreme and unmistakable. I promised myself that as soon as I left the hospital, I would get a grip of myself and re-align with what I was in Thailand to do. Then in the early morning of day seven I woke up, it was still dark, and the clock said around 3.40am. I felt a sticky liquid all over my body. I leaned over and turned on my bedside lamp and I was covered in blood. I suddenly remembered when the doctor said I had a higher chance of dying. It was now day seven and I was covered in blood. My heart started racing and I began to panic. My mind started saying, "You're bleeding to death!" I then looked at my right arm and saw that the drip had come loose and blood was shooting out of my arm. I called the nurse and she plugged it back up. Phew! This was another quick reminder from life. A little nudge to help me remember how valuable my life is.

I left the hospital the next day, alive, determined, and focused on my healing work. I could have seen this event as another dark moment and become a victim. But I knew that there was more to this, much more. Life helped me when I needed it. This kick up the arse was I exactly what I needed, and life was more than willing to assist. However, life does not have to get that severe. We do not have to go through so much pain and suffering to become who we truly are, although for some it is necessary. Even when life seems to be against us, it is actually working for us. We just lack the understanding to see how everything is working in our favour. We are always quick to feel like a victim when life becomes challenging. We seldom think of taking a step back to see what life is trying to show us. We may have to end a relationship, leave a job that is not aligned with our hearts desire, or follow a path that has no guarantees, but feels right in every cell of our being. Life will encourage us by shaking our foundations. This can make our life seem like it is in turmoil, and it is not always easy but it is necessary. A little nudge from life can turn into a shake when we are not paying attention or refusing to change our ways.

We can have little nudges from our intuition to let us know something needs to change. We may ignore these inner nudges, but after a while these little nudges may turn into a push that gives us no choice but to pay attention. We often ignore the little nudges because we are stuck in our comfort zone. We may want something new and different from life but are not willing to adjust or change anything. Life will keep giving us situations to help us get to where we need to be. These situations may turn into the most difficult decisions we have ever had to make. But life knows where we need to be and will do all it can to get us there. It is our unwillingness to leave our comfort zone and feel the uncomfortable feelings of change that keep us where we do not want to be. If we are unwilling to step out of the little box that we have created, how can anything ever change?

THE LITTLE BOX

We all have our comfort zones and within that comfort zone is our 'safe' little reality we have created for ourselves. We dream about living a different life and want to create change, but don't even try to move beyond our comfort zone. We develop behaviours and patterns that are designed to keep us safe but keep us small and unwilling to take positive action. When we deny ourselves the pleasure of being ourselves we suffer, and we carry a fear that by being ourselves we will suffer even more. This is what keeps many of us stuck within the little box that we are trying to break free from. This little box creates a false sense of safety. We think that by hiding and staying small through our fear of being seen for who we truly are, we have less chance of being seen and rejected. What many of us do not realise is that by staying small and acting through fear, we attract what we fear into our lives. Instead of staying safe by staying small, we are doing the opposite.

Our little box is made from fear, and when we believe in fear we allow it to manifest into our lives. This does not mean fear is real. It is just another part of the illusion that we create. Fear is not real, but we make it real when we give energy to it. We have put a lot of trust in fear, believing it is keeping us safe, when all it does is keep us locked in Hell. It may tempt us with mind-made scenarios of things that may happen, and when we believe these stories, we climb back into our little box.

Fear plagues society. It dictates and controls people's lives when they allow it to. But have we been looking at fear with the wrong perception? Can fear be used to help us? I think so. Fear is a signal that we have a belief that is out of alignment with our true nature. A belief like 'I am not good enough' will create fear and resistance when we set out to achieve something. When we become aware of the beliefs that we carry within, we can view fear as the fragrance of these beliefs. This backwards observation can create a healthier understanding of our fearful behaviour. When we fear doing something, it is because we believe that something we don't want to happen, may happen.

Say you want to openly express yourself to a group of people? Why would you feel fear? Could it be that the survival of your conditioned self is reliant on your decision to stay small, weak, and afraid? If you are to realise your true nature through your willingness to go against what any fear is saying, you will soon lose the need to stay small and believe in fear. We wash away all fears when we move towards and through them. We are saying to the fear, "I don't believe in you," and therefore removing them and the limited false sense of self.

This is why it is important to face and move through all fears. Imagine fear as the doorway back to who you are. Would you walk through your fear then? Would you feel the fear to experience the joy that is waiting on the other side of it?

What we fear, we must move towards. It is important not to allow any fear that arises to make its way into your mind. You can feel the fear and then move through it. When we allow fear into our minds, we give it breeding space. It will create a horror show, and all our thoughts will impregnate and feed the fear until it takes over and paralyses us. We are then unable to take any kind of action even if we try.

Fear tempts us back into our little box and is the conditioned self's favourite tool to keep us small and weak. To live fully in our conditioning means we are always living in fear, which in turn means we are never living at all. Even if fear is not fully present and just bubbling away beneath the surface, it will always be a reminder to stay small. But we all have something special to share with the world. Some will find it and share it, and others may not. What creates this separation is the relationship we have with fear, and more importantly, how we allow fear to control and plan our lives for us. Redefining your relationship with fear will allow you to live without limitation in the face of fear. When we do what we fear, the fear will disappear. This is because we are sending signals to the distorted beliefs that there is nothing to be afraid of. This makes the subconscious adjust to the truth.

The greatest fear that I had to face and move through was my deep fear of rejection and abandonment, which appeared in my early 20s. At the time, I did not have a clue why it had appeared, or where it was coming from. So, in my oblivious nature, I allowed it to control my life for many years, which resulted in much pain and suffering. I did what I believed would make my environment accept me rather than ever exploring the idea of doing what I wanted to do. This deeply rooted fear of rejection, abandonment and loss seeped into many areas of my life, including my relationships. I was living within an illusionary limited world that was being influenced by my fear of rejection. It was not until I chose to allow this fear to fully arise that it started to disappear. My decision to stay open when fear was telling me to stay closed allowed the fear to leave. Slowly I felt like I was learning how to walk again. I was choosing to be myself, even if that was met with confusion by others. It was not until I decided to travel the world that I really started to open and show my true colours.

If unobserved, fear will live your life for you, having you be and do things you do not want. The conditioned self will use fear to make you believe that it is you who is afraid. What if it is the conditioned self who is afraid, and is using fear to prevent its annihilation? At our core, we can never feel fear, and this is why we can use it to show us where we need to be. Allow fear to be your guide, rather than allowing it to hold you hostage. To re-define fear means changing our relationship with it, seeing it in a different light, and no longer allowing it to control us. Understanding that fear is a non-tangible and illusionary state of mind will guide you to the realisation that it is not real. Fear only becomes real when we give it energy and act through it. Acting through fear and allowing it to possess our thinking feeds the fear, and it will grow and seem very real.

One person I worked with, called Chris, had a terrible fear of anything that involved change. Whenever he was going to catch a flight, or if he had to travel to another location, he would have a sudden feeling of dread and fear that would overwhelm his whole body. Sometimes he would even vomit. He had no idea why he felt this way whenever he was about to change something in his life. It severely restricted his ability to do what he wanted to do. I worked with him to expose where this fear was coming from. We were taken to a memory from when he was around seven years old and his parents were taking him to football practice. He never enjoyed football, but he wanted to please his parents.

One day on his way to football practice he decided to speak up and say that he did not want to go anymore. His parents did not react in the way that he wanted them to. They told him that he was going to go and that was final. He said to them that he wanted to change what he was doing, as he did not enjoy football. His parents pulled the car over and beat him. In that moment, his subconscious used that experience to create a belief that if he ever wanted to 'change' and do something different, it would result in a beating and danger. His subconscious did not want him to experience any harm; it wanted to protect him. The unfortunate thing was that the subconscious had generalised this experience to classify anything remotely linked with change as a danger. This was why he was afraid of anything that involved change.

I helped Chris look at the truth behind his fear of change, so that he could move through it and let it go. About two weeks later, I bumped into Chris and he had just arrived back from a trip to Malaysia to extend his visa so that he could spend more time in Thailand. I asked him if he felt the usual fear when he was traveling to get his visa extended. He said he hadn't even thought about the fear and realised in that moment that it had vanished. In this case, the subconscious was trying to help Chris by steering him away from any situation that involved change.

I was able to help guide Chris back to the source of his fear, but he would have still been able to move through it himself. How? By staying open to change even though he feared it. By staying open and not fearing fear, we allow it to leave. The challenge is that when we are lost in the illusion we are unaware of how fear may be living our lives for us. We cannot see how our fears and conditioned behaviours are the reason our lives look the way they do. The good news is that we always have help but may have been overlooking it. This help comes through what we see and experience moment to moment. We can use all we see on the outside to point to what we cannot see inside. This is when we must take an honest look at what we may have been avoiding.

PART

4

LIFE IS A MIRROR

"We but mirror the world. All the tendencies present in the outer world are to be found in the world of our body. If we could change ourselves, the tendencies in the world would also change."

~ Mahatma Gandhi

THE ONE AND ONLY PROBLEM

The world we see outside ourselves is nothing more than a projection of a world that we have made real in our minds. When the world we have created becomes challenging, we do all that we can to change it. We seldom think to start with ourselves. When life becomes all consuming, we may ask questions like, 'Why me?', or, 'What have I done to deserve this?'. As difficult as your life may have become, has it ever occurred to you that you may be the one responsible for how it looks?

When I was suffering with persistent health issues, I tried everything I could to treat and alleviate the symptoms. This did not work, and my health stayed the same. It was not until I decided to take a deeper look inside that the symptoms started to fade away, allowing my health to improve. There is always a reason that our lives look the way they do, and we are always the ones responsible. We may think that health issues randomly sprout out of nowhere, like God is punishing us, but there is always an underlying reason and cause. When we find the cause, we can heal it. The same applies to our life circumstances. If you are suffering with persistent unwanted situations, do you keep trying to treat the symptom and change the situation? Or do you dig deep and look at what may be causing the unwanted situations, so that you can heal it, and by doing so, heal your life?

The reason that the plant medicine Ayahuasca is so effective is that it shows you who you are. It also shows you who you are not. An Ayahuasca experience can be like having a big, harsh, honest mirror placed right in front of you showing all the hidden conditioned aspects of yourself. To see who we are not can be painful, as we face the source of the pain we have created for ourselves and others. Upon clear observation of a self that has been sabotaging our entire life, we can let it go. We do not have to drink Ayahuasca to see the conditioned self, as we are having this self shown to us every day. We see this side of 'our self' through the situations that trigger it and bring it to the surface. We can see the fears from which we are operating through the situations we keep experiencing. The repetitive dramas that keep showing up are doing so to help you see who you are choosing to be. All the conditioned aspects of who we are not, that are standing in the way of who we are, will be shown to us through life's mirror.

When we are acting through our conditioning, we are unconsciously creating a world that reflects who we are choosing to be. The structure of the conditioned self is built on fear. When we look at the world through a fearful conditioned version of who we are, the world reflects that fear back to us. Just like wearing sunglasses distorts our view of reality, so does looking at the world through our conditioned eyes. Your reality always mirrors and complements what you believe and feel within. If you believe that the world is a dangerous place, your mind will be wired to selectively seek out danger and miss much of the beauty that is on show. We are always choosing how we want to see the world, and when we choose to see it through the eyes of the conditioned self we suffer. This is because the conditioned self holds the past in front of all that we experience in the present.

When we look at the world through our conditioned eyes, we label and judge. This means that we are not seeing the world at all, we are seeing a fragmented version of what is available. We will then react to the false judgments we have made as though they are true. If we are identified with the conditioned self, we are not seeing or experiencing truth, we are seeing life through the perception of a self that is not true. Everything we could possibly need is at the other side of our incorrect perceptions. Incorrect seeing leads to incorrect living and being, and all the conditioned mind-made errors that we entertain will keep us trapped in that fragmented world. Because our personal reality always gives us a true reflection of who we are choosing to be, we can use everything that happens externally as a mirror to help us see areas that need adjusting internally. This is because anything that is happening on the outside has been created on the inside first. Yes, this means that you are responsible for what is happening to you, and you have the power to change it. When we are acting through the conditioned self, which is layered with limiting beliefs and unresolved emotions, we create a reality to match. We are essentially projecting an accumulation of our past into the present and calling it life.

Some quantum physicists have called reality a hologram, with us as the projectors creating our very own personal reality. Greg Braden, the author of *The Divine Matrix*, says, "In the Divine Matrix, we are the container within which all things exist, the bridge between the creations of our inner and outer worlds, and the mirror that shows us what we have created." Greg Braden is not the only person to point to this understanding of how our reality works. Michael Talbot, the author of *The Holographic Universe*, says, "There is evidence to suggest that our world and everything in it – from a snowflake to a maple tree to falling stars and spinning electrons – are ghostly images, projections." Two of the world's most eminent thinkers – University of London physicists David Bohm, a former protégé of Einstein's and one of the world's most respected quantum physicists, and Stanford neurophysiologist Karl Pribram – believe that the universe itself may be a giant hologram, quite literally a kind of image or construct created, at least in part, by the human mind. As far out as this idea may sound, there are many quantum physicists backing this idea with revolutionary evidence.

Life is a mirror of our beliefs; our beliefs fuel our fears and insecurities, and thus our behaviour and actions. Our beliefs create our reality, and, when we view the world through our conditioned eyes, we see a world that is subject to our conditioned programming. The saying 'seeing is believing' is the wrong way around; a better term would be 'believing is seeing': we see and experience what we believe to be true. This means that we are all experiencing different realities simultaneously, and why one person's perception of the world may differ to how others see and experience it.

Gandhi puts it like this, "Your beliefs become your thoughts. Your thoughts become your words. Your words become your actions. Your actions become your habits. Your habits become your values, and your values become your destiny." What Gandhi is essentially saying is our beliefs create our reality. But not only our beliefs, the actions that follow them. This shows that when we believe, and then act through our beliefs, we empower them, and that allows them to be the source of the life we experience.

I once worked with a woman named Tara. She needed assistance with an anxiety issue, and a fear of people not taking her seriously and abandoning her. When she was a child three of her best friends came to her house to see her. Tara was getting ready to go out and play with them when one of the three girls said, "We came to tell you that we don't want to be your friends anymore." Tara was traumatised, and as a result felt confused and angry. In that moment Tara created the belief, "I am a bad person". She carried this belief with her ever since, and was afraid of getting too close to people as she did not want to re-experience this level of rejection. Tara's belief that she was a bad person was affecting everything that she did and did not do. She became afraid of leaving the house to go food shopping in case anyone spoke to her, or even looked at her. This anxiety and fear, fuelled by her belief of 'I am a bad person' created her reality. It drove her to see only the things that confirmed and justified her belief. She projected this belief out into her life and made it true. Tara's greatest fear was having this belief revealed, so she would do all that she could to not be seen as a bad person, or not to be seen at all. She became a pleaser, and extremely over analytical. What stunned Tara the most was the pattern that ran through her entire life. She told me about at least five different occasions when one friend or another had said, "I don't want to be your friend anymore." She was replaying that childhood rejection over and over because she had not yet processed it and resolved it internally. The reason she kept attracting the same situations was so that she could see her belief that she was a bad person, look at it, and let it go. With a lack of awareness, she could not see how she was creating the reality that she was trying to escape.

The conditioned self is littered with all kinds of different limiting beliefs. When we align with a belief, either positive or negative, we create a reality to match, and this can control our behaviour and decision-making. We can even be carrying beliefs that do not belong to us. This means that we have had beliefs that belong to somebody else passed down to us. We are carrying another person's beliefs, believing them to be true for ourselves. Your beliefs may not be true, but you make them true when you believe them and act through them. A belief only has power when you believe it. If you have a belief that money is bad and dirty, then you will find it hard to make money. If you believe that love brings suffering and pain, you will resist giving and receiving love, and if you believe that you are not good enough, you will not have the motivation to make the first step. When we believe our beliefs, they create our reality, but these beliefs can be seen as true or not true. Some beliefs are true and in alignment with the laws of Nature. Like gravity, for example. If you do not believe in gravity, it does not mean that it will not work, and you would float off into the sky when you step outside. And If you do not believe in oxygen, it does not mean that you will choke when you try to breathe. Other than the beliefs that create the framework for the reality that we live in, we have accumulated many distorted and limiting beliefs that are not true. If you believe that you can or cannot do something, it will be true in the reality that you create.

We all have radically different beliefs that influence how we see the world. We only have to look at the wars that have been created in the name of beliefs, and people who have been executed in the name of beliefs. Indeed, some people can become so entrenched, dogmatic, and determined to stick to their beliefs, they choose to die for them, rather than entertain another viewpoint. Dying for your beliefs does not make them true, far from it, but they are true to the people who are creating their reality through them. We have all been subjected to different kinds of conditioning, which have resulted in different kinds of beliefs. As we see the world one way, somebody else can see it a completely different way, and this can create conflict. But, with a slight shift in perception, and dropping the need to always be right, anything is possible, and any argument or war is avoidable. When we have become accustomed to seeing the world a certain way for most our life, it can be daunting and maybe even frightening to start looking at it differently. The older we grow, the more fixed in our conditioned self we become, and thus in how we believe the world should look. We may begin to think other people are strange for seeing the world differently to how we see it.

We are all creating and living in our own worlds, which operate through our conditioning. To then leave that world, even if that world is bringing a great deal of suffering and unhappiness, can be difficult. During my six years in the British Army, I witnessed many people leave or be discharged. I stayed in contact with some of them and was interested to see how they adapted to what we used to call 'normal life'. Many found it challenging to adapt, after being so reliant on the army. Their routine, having a rank to feel more significant to others, and most of all the camaraderie that was always surrounding them was now gone. They missed their world; army life contained the only things that was real to them, and life on the outside seemed alien. Luckily, I never became heavily reliant on the army, and never really saw army life as my world or reality, so when I left it was an easy transition back into the ‘normal world’. I met many ex-soldiers through my sales work. Some of them were miserable and missed their old life. They had become institutionalised in the army and could not adjust themselves into a reality that was different from the one they had become reliant on.

We always have access to two different realities. The first reality is created when we act through the conditioned self. Even though this may feel like reality, we are living in an illusion, as our life is just a projection of our conditioned programmes. This explains why we all react differently to similar situation. The second reality is the true undistorted reality that runs below the hectic mixture of all the other realities taking place. The reality we view through our conditioned filters will never give us a true representation of what is truly available. What we see is just a reflection of what we hold within. The outer is no different from the inner. If you have been surrounded by violence as a child, you may grow to witness a world that is violent. Does this mean that the world is violent? No, it means that you are seeing what is within you. Just as some people see a world filled with evil, others may see a world filled with beauty, and this shows they are more connected to the beauty within themselves. We always have a choice as to how we see the world. In every moment, we can either follow the guidance of the conditioned self and seek out the darkness, or we can shine our light and see the beauty.

We are all unique individuals who have the right to live how we choose. We do not have to act through beliefs that have been passed down to us from other people. If we act through another person's belief, that means we are acting like another person. We are acting through our conditioning and not being ourselves. We are then creating a reality that is subject to the beliefs, fears, and limitations that have been passed down to us. How others have viewed the world through their beliefs could be the world that you are viewing through your beliefs right now. Does this mean your beliefs are true? Maybe now is a good time to ask yourself what you believe in, and if what you believe feels true to you. How have these beliefs shaped the world that you live in? Are these beliefs supportive or destructive? Whatever your answers are, hopefully you are starting to see that the limiting and challenging situations you have experienced have been created through the programmes you have been operating from. It can be difficult to take full responsibility for how our lives look, but once we do, we empower ourselves and can change ourselves and our world. The world can give you only what you give to it. This is because what we see out there is a projection or what is in here. The trap that many of us fall into is to get lost in what is happening out there and believe that is how our lives are destined to be.

LOST IN THE STORY

The conditioned mind loves a dramatic situation to chew on. This is why it is easy to get lost in the story and fixate on what has happened. “I can’t believe Steve has done this again, I am furious!” “You won’t believe what happened to me last week!” We can get lost in the story without ever paying attention to what the story is pointing to. Look around at the number of people who have something or more importantly somebody to moan about, blaming them for the way they feel.

Imagine Life, dressing itself up as a situation to come and point to those parts of you that need your loving attention; well this is what’s happening. The things that cause us distress may be the only way that we can recognize the parts of ourselves that are out of alignment with who we truly are. When we believe a limiting conditioned programme, act through it, and create a reality to match, we may wonder what has happened. Because we are acting unconsciously on autopilot when the conditioned self is active, we cannot see how we are sabotaging our own lives. Your life is always going to kindly reflect who you are choosing to be through the repetitive situations that you are experiencing. When we are confronted with a challenging situation, we have a tendency to lose ourselves in the situation, allowing them to drain us emotionally. The only reason we suffer when we are faced with a challenging situation is that we choose to believe the beliefs that are being exposed. But everything is helping us, especially challenging situations, and the more we resist these challenges, the more we resist change and the harder life becomes.

Do you think that you can really rearrange your external world so that nothing challenging ever happens? You may even choose to try and run away from life's challenges, move to an exotic part of the world and lock yourself away in the hope that the situations will stop. But they will always find you. We cannot expect life to change until we do. We cannot see a shift in the outer world until we have made a shift in our inner world. And this means working with the situations that life brings.

Life is like having many plates spinning at once. Just as you get them all spinning together, and you think your life is running smoothly, one of the plates falls and smashes. The plates represent the different areas of our life. We may feel as though we have our lives running smoothly when suddenly something unexpected happens and we are faced with another unwanted situation. The extent of the situations may vary, but we are always being shown conditioned aspects of ourselves that are hiding within. We must be comfortable knowing that plates are going to fall, and sometimes smash.

Looking back at the darkest parts of my life shows me when I was suffering the most. I was resisting seeing the conditioned aspects of myself that life's situations were pointing to. But what if there are no situations? What if life is just happening, and we fragment it into situations and challenges based on the conditioned limitations that are being exposed. We then say that something terrible happened, and maybe it did. But maybe what also happened was deep healing. Would you then see that as an unwanted situation?

Instead of losing ourselves in the story we can look at what the situation and story is pointing to. This allows us to remove the cause from its source and eliminate the repeating unwanted situations. We are then able to let go of our inner programs that will alter our external reality. Just the same as when you are watching a DVD and you don't like the movie, what do you do? Do you change the DVD for something that you do like, or do you try to find a new TV so that you can change the screen? You may even become angry at the TV screen and punch it for showing you something you do not like. But the TV screen was just doing its job in showing you what was on the DVD. Just like life is showing you what is in your mind.

Let's say that you were traumatized by an event in your childhood. Perhaps you witnessed your parents arguing, and that made you feel sad, lonely, and afraid. Fast forward 30 some years, and you seem to keep attracting relationships that make you feel sad, lonely, and afraid. If you take your attention away from the drama within the relationship, and instead focus on what the relationship is trying to tell you about yourself, you can allow the pain of the past to leave. You are inviting the drama, and so-called unwanted situations, to help you see what you cannot. How else can we expose what is hiding deep within, unless we have it shown to us? Life knows the perfect person and situation to help expose what needs to be removed.

I SEE IN YOU WHAT I HAVE IN ME

A strong reaction towards another person is an indication that we are carrying the same, or similar conditioning. Our perceptions are projections created through what we have inside. When we say to someone else, "You are so controlling!", what we may be saying is, "I am so controlling!". We attract other people into our lives who mirror who we are choosing to be, or parts of our conditioned selves that we cannot see. Let's say that you keep attracting people into your life who moan and groan about their life. This frustrates you, and you go away and moan and groan about the people who moan and groan. Sound familiar? These people are showing us aspects of our own conditioned behaviours. Just like a person who gossips about people that gossip. Or somebody who gets angry at angry people. We are always being shown ourselves through life's mirror.

I remember being in relationships, and amid an argument telling my partner all the things that I disliked about her, only to now know that list was really things I disliked about myself. We may also witness this in other people's behaviours. Many years ago, I was in my friend's car as we drove down the motorway. Suddenly, the traffic slowed down to a standstill. Once it had started to speed up again, we realised there was an accident up ahead, and the drivers in front had all slowed down to have a look. My friend, who was driving, became extremely angry when he realised the reason for our long wait was because of the other drivers' decision to look at the accident. He carried on cursing for the next 10 or so minutes. Eventually the traffic returned to its normal flow. It was then our turn to pass the accident, and sure enough, my friend slowed down and had a look, doing the very thing that he had been so angry about. My friend was becoming angry at others for things that were clearly within him.

Situations that keep repeating themselves, and the way we react to them, are obvious pointers to what needs to be looked at. Once we expose what we need to see, and realise we are the ones creating what we do not want, we can begin to make the steps towards letting go of what does not serve us. It is easy to understand intellectually that we are the ones that create everything that happens to us, and then forget when presented with a challenging situation. We may initially fall back into our habitual behaviour of blaming others for how we feel. It is important that we do not lose sight of how we are fully responsible for what we experience.

Our relationships provide us with the clearest mirrors to work with. Everyone we attract into our lives is a mirror through which we can observe the conditioned self. Every single one of our relationships: our friends, families, children, neighbours, co-workers, and our romantic partners all reflect specific parts of us. I sometimes refer to the conditioned self as our shadow side or our blind spot. This is because we cannot see the conditioned self when it is driving our behaviour, which is why we need to have it shown to us by other people. Within our shadow side lies all the parts of us that we do not wish to see or cannot see. Our fears, insecurities, and distorted beliefs all dwell in our shadow side. We can try to escape or suppress them, but they will always make themselves known through the people we attract. Not only will people mirror our shadow side, but we will mirror theirs. Relationships present the perfect opportunity to see conditioned aspects of ourselves.

We can never really escape our past unless we are willing to see and release the conditioned aspects of who we think we are. This is why all interactions with others are valuable, as they can show us what is standing in the way of truth.

All relationships are of mutual benefit, even if it does not always seem that way. We can spend countless hours talking about all the negative things that another person has done, but what we are revealing are all the things that we dislike about ourselves.

Relationships can be extremely powerful if we are willing to allow them to show us things about ourselves that we have shied away from for many years. This means that the conditioned self will be triggered and brought to the surface. Being emotionally connected with somebody means that they can trigger you on a deeper level than anybody else. This is why relationships can be the perfect way to help us let go of what is standing in our way to be our true selves. Two people may come together, trigger each other, blame each other, and never make any real progress. But two people with a little more awareness may come together and trigger one another's conditioning and be able to work through their old pain and transform. Unless you learn to face your own shadows, you will keep being haunted by them. People that show up in your life and really know how to push your buttons are just showing you who you are not, so that you can remember who you are.

You are not your conditioned limitations, which means you are not who you think you are. To stay open to life, and what it is showing us means we allow ourselves to move back to our truth. All that you are searching for is beyond the false identification you have made about yourself. We must allow these false concepts of who we think we are to be taken away to reveal the truth of who we are. We do this by peeling away the layers of the conditioned self, to allow our light to shine through.

PART

5

PEELING AWAY THE LAYERS

"Being a candle is not easy, in order to give light, one must first burn."

~ Rumi

NON-REACTION

When a situation comes along and pokes us to reveal our conditioning, we are waking up these layers and allowing them to come to the surface to be seen. Once we see them and acknowledge that they are just our past conditioning, we can let them go. We then have fewer layers in the way of our truth. One thing that hinders the natural peeling away process is our reaction to the situations that are revealing our conditioned layers. When we react against situations and people, we are resisting and avoiding the natural transformational process. We react against life, as though we know how it should be. The intelligence of life is greater than anything the conditioned mind could ever comprehend. Why even try to resist what life brings? To transform, we must get ourselves out of the way, and drop our conditioned reactive behaviours. We must go with life's flow, rather than trying to swim upstream. And we do this by doing the opposite to what we have always done, we allow life to be as it is without reacting to it.

Non-reaction shows that you are accepting what is, as it is, without trying to fix, change, or rearrange it. Non-reaction is choosing to be your true self rather than the conditioned self. This does not mean that you want your life to be as it is, it means that you accept the way your life is, know that you are exactly where you need to be, and trust that you are being guided back home.

Being triggered is a blessing, as it shows us parts of our conditioning that we would not normally be able to see. It may seem that something negative just happened, as we feel emotions that we do not want to feel. These unwanted emotions are part of the conditioned self, blocking our ability to be who we are. What most people do when they are triggered is react. It seems to be inherent in society to react to people and events that trigger our conditioning. The word ‘react’, has two parts to it. Re means again. Act means act. React literally means to re-act the same situations over and over again. Unwanted situations cannot go away until we let go of what they are exposing. Instead, we don’t notice the conditioned self behind our reaction. We seldom think to look at what is making us react, and so we do what we have always done, react. Upon our observation and without any identification to what has been triggered, we let it go. This may sound easy, and it certainly can be, but we make it difficult for ourselves when we identify with what has been triggered. To be triggered is only the first step in peeling away the conditioned self. We must then make sure that we can be with what has been triggered, with no identification, and without allowing our thinking to be fueled by what has been triggered. By doing this we are not allowing the conditioned self to hold onto anything when it is revealed. We are creating an open space to allow whatever has been triggered to be peeled away and leave.

To react is to stay in the same place and choose not to be at one with our truth. We are then allowing what has been triggered to re-establish itself through us. The conditioned self has then taken you over. Through a reactive behaviour, we are not taking responsibility for the way we feel. We are reacting and blaming the trigger rather than looking at what the trigger has triggered, which is of upmost importance. When we take our attention away from the story we are left with the emotion, and by letting go of the unresolved emotion that usually fuels conditioned behaviours, we are moving closer to our truth. This is the beginning of true transformation. We are not our emotions, so when they are shown to us we can allow them to pass through without trying to cling to them or suppress them. Unresolved emotions need to come up and leave, because they block what is real. When these emotions are triggered and come to the surface to leave, and we choose to react, we are not only acting them out, but we are making them stronger. We then create a cycle of never-ending situations that keep coming back, triggering the same unresolved emotions. In the East, they call this Karma, but I suppose in the West we could also call it ignorance. Look at the situations that keep repeating in your life. Think back to a situation that made you feel angry, sad, or maybe even guilty. How did you handle this situation? Did you react? Did you become what you were made to feel? Did you act out the emotion and fall back into limited behavioural patterns? We may think that by reacting we are in control of life and the situations that life presents, but reaction only ever keeps us stuck within the same unwanted situations and behaviours.

When life happens, as it always will, and reveals a conditioned layer, we can peel away this layer and let it go. How do we do this? By choosing *not* to react. We have two choices when faced with a situation. We either act out what has been triggered or become aware of it. This simple and yet extremely powerful practice may not be so easy to execute at first. This is because we are going against deeply ingrained behaviours. Take a look around and see how most of society blames and reacts to what life presents them. This is unconscious behaviour, and when everybody else is doing it, it seems normal to be doing it too.

We must be willing to adopt a new way of living that does not conform to how society acts and chooses to live. We believe that complaining, blaming, and reacting is normal and justified. All this kind of behaviour keeps us separated from our truth. But the only way out of our conditioned limitations is to face and move through them.

When we react, we strengthen the conditioned self, which means that when we choose non-reaction, we not only weaken it, but dissolve it. Imagine that you could fully trust that all situations, people, and triggers were happening to help you. How would you respond to them? Would you curse them, react against them, or become grateful for them? If you are serious about discovering who you truly are, you must be serious about allowing what needs to happen to happen. What you think must happen, or how it should happen may be going against how it needs to happen.

Neuroscience has shown that a behaviour is made up of neural networks. Dr Joe Dispenza talks about this in his book *Breaking the Habit of Being Yourself*. One of his catch phrases in it is, 'What no longer fires together, no longer wires together'. When we think a thought, or play out a certain behaviour, we send an electric current through the neural networks, and this keeps them alive and active. But when we choose not to react and act out a conditioned behaviour, we no longer send the same electric current, and thus no longer need the conditioned behaviour, allowing it to detach and fade away. We are then literally letting go of who we used to be. It seems that science itself is now showing that, by choosing to be ourselves instead of reacting through our conditioned behaviours, we are disconnecting from them to move back into our natural state of being. By living a non-reactive lifestyle and working to reverse the conditioning process, you are allowing yourself to change.

All situations that arise are a way for us to see what has been making us react. Reacting is a clever ploy the conditioned self uses to not have itself seen – urging us to lash out and keep our focus outwards, rather than looking inwards directly at it. This keeps our attention away from the one and only problem.

When 'you' think that you feel angry or sad, and feel the need to react, it is not you, it is the conditioned version of you. It tricks you into believing that it is you, and because of this you believe that you have been hurt and want to retaliate against whatever hurt you. This cycle of reactivity can last a lifetime, as we perpetuate the heavy baggage of the past through unwanted situations in the present. It is time for us to turn the tables and play the conditioned self at its own game. We can use the situations that trigger it as an opportunity to see it. Do not fear looking right at it, as when you do, you take away its power and ability to influence your behaviours.

We always know when we have acted through our truth rather than acting out old conditioned behaviours. We know this because it feels right. Think back to a time when you were faced with a situation that tempted you to act out the emotions that had been triggered. Maybe you intuitively knew the situation would turn ugly if you did so, and chose another, calmer, more controlled and real way. Maybe you chose not to react. How did you feel afterwards? Good? It's quite simple to know when you have acted through your truth as it feels right, and you know inside that your actions were coming from a different place. You can also see the difference in how the situations unfold, with grace and ease. What do you do if you don't react? You do nothing! I cannot express how powerful non-reaction is when faced with a challenging situation. We always feel that we should do something, we should instantly defend or justify ourselves, we should make the person who triggered our emotions feel what we are feeling. But who is defending itself? The conditioned self defends itself, but when we do nothing, we are doing everything. This is because we are giving ourselves time to find clarity through the foggy limiting emotions that have been triggered. You will notice that once you have clarity of mind, the right course of action will come to you, or the situation will have taken care of itself. It still amazes me when I am faced with a testing situation, and don't act out what has been triggered, and choose to stay calm, I find myself watching the situation blossom into a peaceful resolution.

The temptation to fall into the grip of the conditioned self and react can be challenging to say the least. When we choose not to react, we can see the conditioned self, and many aspects of who we have believed we are. It takes courage to have an honest look at ourselves amid a situation that has triggered powerful feelings within us. This is what separates those who truly want change in their lives, from those who don't. The latter may say they do, but unconsciously choose to act the same way and hold onto hope that one day their life will miraculously change. But miraculous change will never happen unless we are willing to be radically honest about why we feel the way we feel.

Look at it this way, the only thing standing in the way of us being ourselves is our conditioning. If you aren't sure you can be bothered to put in the effort required for letting go of the aspects of yourself that hinder your ability to be the true you, my advice is this: Keep acting the same way that you have always acted. React to the same situations that will keep you biologically connected with the same self. Do what you have always done and act as you have always acted. And by doing so, I can assure you that you will be able to experience the same unwanted situations and limited state of being. However, if you are serious about creating a lasting shift and pure connection with yourself, then adopting a non-reactive lifestyle, whilst being aware of what is being triggered, will begin to dissolve the old conditioned self, allowing your truth to be revealed and expressed.

There is a great deal of stigma attached to showing our emotions. So much so, that we would rather suffer and pretend that all is well, than allow whatever emotions need to be felt and let go of. What defines a strong person? Is it when we can put on a brave face in challenging situations? True strength is when we are humble enough to feel our emotions without judgment. We are not weak if we feel sadness, anger or any other challenging emotion, far from it. Emotions are energy in motion, they come and go. When we allow this natural flow to happen, we are flushing out the past to reveal our truth.

In the toughest moments, choose to embrace what has been triggered, even when your mind is telling you to get angry and verbally lash out and blame those who have 'hurt you'. Does lashing out every really get us anywhere? Does it ever make us feel better or resolve the conflict that we are trying to escape? True change comes when we can be with any emotion that has been triggered and allow it to be processed and transmuted back into our energy system. When we do this, we can instantly feel calmer and centred. Choosing to embrace anything that life brings with this attitude is a true warrior's spirit. Don't choose to do what people around you are doing and think that this is healthy, because it isn't. Suppression of our emotions only leads to more pain.

DON'T SHOOT THE MESSENGER

It can be tempting to blame other people for the way they make us feel. Your initial response to somebody may be 'you made me feel this way!' But rather than pointing the finger and saying 'you', we can come back to ourselves and say 'I'. 'I made me feel this way'. Whenever we blame, we are stoking the fire of conflict. Saying how we feel without pointing the finger at the other person brings more control into the conversation. We can then express how we feel without perpetuating and losing ourselves in the emotion.

I am a highly sensitive person and have always expressed how I feel. I have been told on many occasions 'you are too sensitive'. I used to think that this meant there was something wrong with me, and always felt different from others. During my time in the army, I became increasingly angry with the control and not being allowed to express my emotions. The anger within me was being repeatedly triggered, but I was fueling it with more anger because I had no outlet to safely express how I felt. I was expected to be a robot, and just do what I was told to do. It took some time after leaving the army to learn to express how I felt without becoming lost in the emotion. I realised this holds the foundation for healthy and transparent communication. There is so much power in being able to be with and share how we feel, even when what we feel has been triggered by somebody else.

The more that you can be aware of how you are reacting and feeling in certain situations, the more you can see what needs to be let go of. You can have conditioning triggered and brought to the surface. And instead of having the awareness to see it for what it is and letting it go, you may blame and judge the person who triggered it. You then label that person as 'a bad person' and put them in a box that you have created. We are then holding onto what is being revealed. We live in a reactive society and people generally seem to have somebody to blame and moan about, hold a grudge against or generally dislike. Does this mean that everybody is wrong, and we are right? When somebody says or does something that upsets you, Is It theIr fault? Instead of focusing our attention on what a person has done or said to make us feel a certain way, we need to be looking at why we feel that way.

Blame is a great way to deflect feeling any pain or discomfort. We use blame instead of self-reflection, and in doing so invite situations to come back in a slightly different form. We can become stuck within a way of living that we hate when we are unwilling to change. Remember Bill Murray in the movie *Groundhog Day*? He was waking up and living the same day over and over. The way that he was able to break this cycle was to accept his life situation and change his behavior towards it. He was able to fully accept what he was resisting and, in the process, transform his day and himself. He awoke the next day and could carry on living his life, a changed man. We too can become stuck in the same situations that trigger the same feelings that point to the same conditioning. We blame when we are afraid to look within. When we realise that we are responsible for the situations that have turned up in our life, we can choose to change them by changing ourselves. When we point the finger of blame, we are avoiding taking any responsibility. We are choosing to stay exactly where we are.

When one finger is pointing out, there are always three fingers pointing back, telling us to investigate our feelings, rather than the person whom we are blaming for triggering them.

You may, for example, dislike somebody and say things like, 'I hate John, he is so selfish'. You can switch this and see that it could be a reflection and a projection, 'I hate myself as I am selfish'. Maybe John is the person whom you have attracted into your life to show you a part of yourself that you do not like. What creates growth and transformation is how much we can see through what the person has done and discover what they were trying to help us see within ourselves.

Life's mirror shows us who we are being in any moment, because we attract situations that push our buttons, triggering aspects of the conditioned self, which come to the surface for us to see. I call the people whom we attract to show us our conditioned self, our messengers. Our messengers help us see our conditioned behaviours, including the emotions we have been avoiding, and the beliefs that have been driving our behaviours. We attract people into our lives to bring these aspects to the surface, no matter how well we think we have hidden them.

Think about the people in your life who know how to push your buttons. It may be friends or family members. We may avoid these people – they always seem to know what to say and do to show us parts of the conditioned self that we do not want to see. We always have two options. We can blame the other person for how we feel and keep hold of our conditioned limitations. Or we can forget about what the person did (the trigger) and focus on what we feel (the emotion) and, in the process, let it go.

Let's say you have many layers of anger hidden within, but pretend to be zen and calm, you will still attract situations and people to trigger that anger. You can blame and point the finger and truly believe you are a calm person and the only reason you are responding with anger is because of the situation. You may truly believe that the emotions you are feeling are the other person's fault. The truth is that you are feeling the layers of anger that were already within you.

Our messengers may make us feel like they are inflicting pain on us, when in fact they are revealing it to us. All pain that we feel was already within us and is part of the conditioned self. When you are triggered by your messengers and feel an undesirable emotion, you are exactly where you need to be in that moment. If somebody says something to make you feel sad, why do you feel sad? If somebody does not let you out at a junction when you are driving, and that makes you feel angry, why do you feel angry? 'How dare you! Look what you have done! You have made me extremely angry! It's your fault!' Is this true?

When the conditioned self has been wounded, it wants to retaliate. Even if somebody looks you in the eyes and says, 'You are a bad person', does that mean that it's true, and you need to defend yourself? Does it mean that you must feel like a bad person? You may be carrying conditioning that you are a bad person, and maybe you needed somebody to come and show it to you, so you can let it go. You may have the emotion triggered, but you do not have to identify with it and make it part of who you are. You are then detached from what has been triggered and can watch it dissolve. When you choose to believe what has been triggered, you are keeping hold of it, and this means that you need another painful situation to come and show you who you believe you are. What people say to you or about you can only hurt you when you believe it to be true.

Instead of thinking, 'Why did she do that to me?', we could be asking, 'Why did what she do bother me so much? Let's investigate' Curiosity, rather than condemnation, will enable you to resolve and release all of what is being shown to you. Taking this line of enquiry will show you all the other times that similar things have happened. Bringing our attention and awareness inwards brings control and strength. Keeping our attention outwards through our reactive behaviours keeps us trapped in fear and weak.

Any interaction with another person is as an opportunity for transformation. We can go around in circles for the rest of our lives, trying to change someone else to make ourselves feel better. Or we can take responsibility for what is being shown to us. The next time you are thinking of pointing your finger to blame or shoot your messenger, thank them, as they are helping you remember who you are.

RIDING OUT THE STORM

Being deeply triggered can feel like being in the middle of a storm. This emotional storm can make us do and say things that are not in line with our true nature. The trick is to allow the emotional storm to pass without getting lost in it. Getting caught in a storm can do some damage, but, when you reach the eye of the storm, you find peace, and can allow the storm to pass. Our emotional storm dissipates through our non-reaction. If we step out into the emotional storm, we will be blown around by it, and become what has been triggered. We all have different degrees to which we can be triggered. We brush off some things and forget about them almost instantly. Others get to us a bit more. And then there's that one special button that, when pressed, makes us lose our shit. When that button gets pressed, it feels as though our lives are crumbling down around us, but this is a wonderful opportunity to let go of the deep unresolved emotions that steal our ability to feel true happiness.

I read an article in a newspaper many years ago. This man was driving to work one morning when another driver pulled out in front of him, and nearly hit his car. Infuriated, the man overtook the other car, and stopped. The other driver had to stop too. The first driver dragged the second one out of his car and beat him to death. Then, once he had calmed down, he sat and waited for the police to arrive and arrest him. This man's layers of unresolved emotion had built up and up until he had burst at the seams, making him act in a way that he would not have done if he had allowed himself to feel and then let go of his emotions in a controlled and safe way. He became lost within his emotional storm, and instead of breathing through it and finding his centre, he acted it out, and committed murder. We have all lost it at some point in our lives, and afterwards thought, 'Why on earth did I do that?' But if we find our centre, our eye of the storm, we can watch and witness as the drama dissolves. The eye of the storm is peaceful and calm, just like our centre. Storms will pass through our lives to assist in our awakening, but we choose whether we stay in the eye of the storm (our centre) or to step out into the storm (challenging situations). Finding your centre enables you to withstand any situation. You are then allowing the peeling away process to happen without any resistance.

We all have that place within that is never rattled, stressed or sad. No matter how tough life becomes, it stays still and quiet. You can access this part of yourself right now by closing your eyes and taking three deep breaths into the centre of your chest and bringing your focus to that point. After you have finished with the breaths keep your focus and attention on this area of your body. Feel any sensations and the calm presence that emanates from this point. This is your centre, the place that you always have access to no matter how challenging life's situations become.

The way to recognize that something has caught you off guard and pulled you out of your center is you will find yourself feeling easily irritated, and not grounded. This does not mean you have failed; it is part of the peeling away process. You may be triggered by something that's just happened, or by remembering something from the past, or by something you think is coming up in the future. Before you know it, you are lost in a flood of limiting emotions. You will learn to see the self that has pulled you out of alignment. Perhaps you spot the series of thoughts created around a situation, or an unresolved emotion that you became. These are all part of the conditioned self's desire to make you identify with it. Just the seeing of that self is enough to bring you back in alignment. By doing this, you are standing in the eye of your storm until it passes. When the storm eventually does pass, it will take layers of the conditioned self with it.

Once a so-called negative situation passes, the dust has settled, and we have calmed down, we can see the situation for what it was all along. When we are looking at a situation through unresolved emotions, it makes the situation something else, usually something negative. This only perpetuates the emotion that has been triggered. However, if we give time to any situation before reacting to it, we allow it to unfold as it needs to. I'm sure that we have all been embroiled in an argument fueled by our unresolved emotional layers, taking it in turns to sling insults at each other, until one person hurts the other more and 'wins' the argument. An argument can last for days, and sometimes years, with the two participants not backing down or admitting defeat. But is there any power in being right all the time? True power resides in admitting when you are wrong and being able to defuse any situation before it turns ugly. This does not mean that you always have to say you were in the wrong. It means that you notice when you have an opportunity to stop an argument in its tracks. Our minds may say things like, 'What are you doing? You should be telling her how she made you feel, she has insulted you,' The mind will try to re-mind you of what it thinks you should be doing. If you believe this, the mind will trick you into reacting and identifying with your conditioning. To not need to react means that you are open to feeling whatever needs to come up and out.

Be aware of how you feel moment to moment. You may notice that at times you feel more distracted, anxious, and fidgety than normal. You may feel like you are rushing to check your phone more often, or just needing something to do as you feel restless. This is a sign that something needs to be released. When we sit and allow ourselves to be with what we are feeling, instead of needing to distract ourselves, we allow the emotions to leave. When an emotional storm comes into your life, stay still and silent within, as you watch the storm pass and take what it needs. What may seem like chaos going on outside and inside is part of your peeling away process. If you can stay as the watcher and trust that all is happening as it needs to, then you can allow 'yourself' to be taken. It is then up to you to allow it to leave. Do not hold onto what the storm wants to take off your hands, to leave you lighter and with a deeper sense of peace.

Processing emotions has nothing to do with thinking. Thinking and emotions do not mix well. Just like adding oil into water. When you allow an emotion to enter your mind, you will try to understand the emotion. This is like trying to explain to a friend what love is. It is impossible to explain or understand an emotion on a conceptual level. Emotions are to be felt not thought. I remember having many sessions with people, particularly men, who had become detached from their emotions. They were always trying to think about how they felt. Whenever I noticed they were becoming emotional during a session I would ask 'How do you feel right now' and their reply would be 'I think I feel….' We cannot think to figure out how we feel, we feel to feel how we feel. To do this we must become more self-aware. Aware of how we have been avoiding feeling certain emotions. This awareness will also show how the conditioned self wants us to react to certain situations. Rather than not having any control and being taken over as soon as any situation is presented, we have the awareness to see the temptation and choose not to react. We then become more aware, through our desire to be more aware.

THE WATCHER

You are the awareness, the container in which everything appears and disappears, comes, and goes. All situations, thoughts, and emotions that manifest within awareness are not who or what you are. You are the witness of all that appears and disappears. To know and live this truth brings instant peace. This is because you no longer identify with what appears within awareness. Instead you allow all that appears and disappears to happen without the need to change it. The conditioned self is an illusionary state of being that relies on your engagement with it to keep it alive. We relinquish the conditioned self when we no longer participate with it. Instead of being pulled from left to right by all that arises within awareness, we let it happen with no need to try and change anything. This makes non-reaction effortless, as the one that is reacting is the conditioned self and not you. How can we react when we are not identified with the one that reacts? This takes awareness and the ability to stand behind and see the conditioned self for what it truly is, a fictitious sense of self, nothing more. Non-reaction is then mixed with dis-identification as we know that we are not what has been triggered. We watch the conditioned self when it has been triggered, instead of defending, justifying, or reacting. Upon our observation, we are peeling away what has been shown to us. True transformation comes when we choose not to identify and act out what has been triggered and brought to the surface. When we feel the conditioned self tempting us to fall back into identification, we can choose to just watch it. We feel the conditioned self slowly diminish as we refuse to identify with it.

Being the watcher means that you can watch what is happening like a spectator, rather than being caught up in what is happening. When you first start practicing this new approach, you may only have a second or two before the conditioned behaviour takes you over. The pull of our conditioned mind can be strong and tempting. However, after you have been watching instead of reacting for a while, you will feel the pull decrease and the temptation weaken. There is a huge amount of power in observing the conditioned self instead of acting it out. This is not something that you do for just 30 minutes per day like meditation. It is to be done whenever you are conscious. Your goal is to be able to spot whatever wants to come and steal your awareness. This means observing everything the mind presents to you. When my mind was busier than it is now, I would imagine my thoughts on a TV or cinema screen. My mind would be hectic, but instead of becoming caught up in my thoughts, or trying to stop them, I would place them onto the cinema screen and imagine that I was sat in the cinema alone, watching the thoughts and eating popcorn. This helped my mind understand that the thoughts did not belong to me, any more than if I were watching a Superman movie believing I was him.

I see the conditioned mind as one big distraction that is always trying to get our attention. Becoming afraid of our thoughts and emotions, and trying to avoid and fight against them, does not work. Trying to run away or suppress our thoughts only gives them strength. Instead we invite them up to be seen or felt. We watch everything that happens with complete detachment. This creates a separation between us and the conditioned self. We then notice a gap has been created and this will bring a feeling of liberation. Dis-identification from our incessant thinking can also bring a burst of energy. This is understandable as our thinking burns up our energy like a furnace burning wood. This is especially true of negative thinking and our identification with it, which leaves us feeling mentally and physically lethargic.

This gap between you and your conditioned self becomes larger the longer you can dis-associate and dis-identify with it. There is a huge difference between being the observer of your thinking and being taken over by the thinking so that you believe you are the one doing the thinking. The conditioned self will use any trick it can to take back control and make you believe that it is you and you are it. Any memories from the past can be used to make you realign with your conditioning. Vigilance is vital as we are creating a clear discernment between who we are and who we are not.

To observe and dis-identify with our conditioning means that we are moving away from it, disregarding it, and seeing it as obsolete. This allows you to have a different approach to life and a healthier relationship with yourself and others. You are then no longer bound by your conditioning. You can be the way you want to be and not the way the conditioned self wants you to act. This is a beautiful process that will have you marveling at how different you have become. The truth is that you are not becoming different, you are just forgetting who you thought you were and remembering who you are and always have been.

PART

6

THE REUNION

"Three things cannot be long hidden: The sun, the moon and the truth."

~ Buddha

THE LIGHT WITHIN

There is a light that shines through us all. This light goes beyond our profession, personality, body and what we regard as the 'self'. On the deepest level, this light is who or what we are, this light is our truth. There are many different names to describe who we are: the source, our higher self, god, consciousness, awareness, love. But words, labels, concepts, or ideas can only point, and cannot really explain who we are. As children, we are at one with our light, and this explains why life is magical. The world that we experience when we are children does not disappear, it is always on show, but we overlook it. To overlook our true reality means we are also overlooking the truth of who we are. And our truth holds everything we could possibly need, and more. So how do we access this truth? By doing what we did when we were children, but this time in reverse. Instead of learning how not to be our true selves and adopting a conditioned self, we unlearn the conditioned self and remember how to be our true selves.

But before we move on, let's do a quick recap of what we have covered so far.

Part 1 explained how as children we all are connected to our truth, and then taken away from it by our conditioning.

Part 2 investigated the consequences of our conditioning, and how we adopt the beliefs of a separate conditioned self – the identification with this self being what keeps us away from our true self.

Part 3 looked at how the identification with a conditioned self means we are living in an illusionary world. The longer and deeper that we identify with this false self, the more we become lost in the illusion.

Part 4 started to look at ways out of this illusion. We can find the exit by using life's mirror to show us who we are choosing to be. This is when we start to take full responsibility for how our life looks.

Part 5 showed how we can see and release layers of the limited conditioned self, to reveal our true limitless self through a practice of non-reaction to whatever life brings.

Now we have arrived at *Part 6* and will remember how to be ourselves again.

SEEING THE TRUTH IN OTHERS

Choosing to only see the light in others means that we are reminding them of their innate power and truth. This is the meaning of true intimacy, as when we see the truth in others we recognize it in ourselves. The word intimacy then becomes into-me-I-see. When we choose to only see the truth in others, it acts as an invitation for them to express who they truly are. And by seeing the light in others, we illuminate it in ourselves. The conditioned self would only have us see the 'bad' in others, choosing to condemn all that they say and do. The conditioned self only wants to see itself in other people and hate them just like it hates itself. A good gauge that we can use to see how connected we are to our light, is to be aware of how we either celebrate the light in others or condemn their darkness. When we are faced with a challenging situation, and with another person's darkness, we have two choices. We can react towards their darkness with our darkness, or we can shine our light and choose to only see the light in them.

To only see a person's light is the true meaning of forgiveness, as we are looking past what we once believed somebody did to us, or anything we dislike about them. We are realizing that it was not them that did anything at all, it was their conditioned self. We are also realizing that when we see and react to something we dislike in them, we are not connected to our truth, and keeping hold of what we do not like about ourselves. To see the light and truth in another means we see past all of what they did, knowing that they did not do anything, and in the process, releasing our conditioned limitations. When Jesus was being crucified he cried out, 'Forgive them for they know not what they do'. What did he mean by this? He was practicing forgiveness by showing the people that were nailing him to the cross were doing so unconsciously and acting through the conditioned illusion of who they believe they were. To forgive is to be free. This may sound like a difficult task for those who have been hurt by another, but let's be honest, who hasn't. Can you think of a person that you dislike and maybe do not want to forgive? What do you think you are gaining by not forgiving that person? What do we think we are achieving by choosing to hurt ourselves through a practice of non-forgiveness?

Part of my experience in Peru was to learn forgiveness. In my Ayahuasca experiences, I was shown many different people that I had not yet forgiven. I was amazed by some of the people I saw in my mind. Old bosses, family members, friends, and people that I had some past altercation with. One person that I faced in my mind was Shaun, the man that murdered my mother. I was shown how he had been acting out the anger, evil and pain that he believed he was. But I also saw the person that was behind this pain, I saw his truth. In that moment I had a decision to either hate him and choose to hate myself or forgive him and free myself. Even though I only had vague memories of what he did and of him as a person, I knew that the anger and sadness I felt inside would be released through my forgiveness. This was not an easy experience as this man brought pain not only to me, but my entire family and many others. I felt that if I forgave him I was being disloyal to my family. I decided to look past what he had done and focus only on his light. I felt so much space open within myself, like I had just let go of a block of concrete that had been hidden in my stomach and chest. I felt anger, sadness, and darkness that I did not know was within me disappear. This experience also showed me how, when we think we should hold a grudge against somebody else, we are holding it against ourselves, no matter what they have done to us. When we think holding a grudge out of pride will somehow hurt another person, we are choosing to carry around our own pain, refusing to let it go.

When we are in a new relationship, we are on our best behaviour and show our truth to each other, just like a peacock showing off its colourful feathers. We naturally see the best in each other, and this is what we call love, the merging of truth. As we progress deeper into our relationship, we start to relax and reveal aspects of our conditioning that were not initially on show. This is when the conditioned self is showing itself. When this happens, it can make the person you are in a relationship with seem completely different to whom you originally met. "If only I had a receipt for when I first purchased this relationship, I would take him back to the shop and swap him for something better!" But are we really seeing a different person, or are we only choosing to see and condemn the conditioned aspects of that person? Even though we may think it is always the other person that has changed and is now showing their 'issues', we seldom seem to think that we could be showing ours. When one person presents their conditioned self, and the other person reacts, they are also being their conditioned self. You then have two people caught in their conditioning, blaming each other for how they are being made to feel. When this happens, we may choose to end the relationship and jump to the next one. We may end up in a relationship that 'ticks all the boxes' and maybe it does. But this can also be a relationship that involves zero growth. A challenging relationship might be exactly what we need to see and release our past pain to remember our truth. To see the truth in another person, no matter what they present to you, means that you are not only going through your own transformation, but you are creating space for them to go through theirs.

We can see the truth in everybody we meet, not just in intimate relationships. We can practise seeing the truth in friends, family members and people at work and people we pass in the street. Whenever we are faced with a situation that pulls our attention towards another person's conditioned self, tempting us to judge through our conditioning, we can see past it and choose only to see their truth and light. Rather than judging and condemning those who we think have done something wrong or bad, we can choose to relinquish any judgments. By doing this, we are choosing the light over the dark and bringing our awareness back to what is real. When we are drawn to something somebody did to us that hurt and cannot seem to shake it off and find ourselves judging that person, it is a good opportunity to question why what they did hurt. Are we feeling angry at them or at ourselves? Are we really seeing something we dislike about them or something about ourselves? The forgiveness that you embody when you see past another person's pain creates a transformation in you and them. And when you see your friend, boyfriend, girlfriend, husband, wife, brother or sister, or anybody else that you are emotionally connected with blossom, you will witness the magic power of forgiveness for yourself. Forgiveness then becomes allowing people to be just as they are without the need to change them or condemn their behaviour. Many people believe that to forgive somebody means to just utter the words 'I forgive you' and then poof! All is forgiven. I'm afraid there is more to it than that. We must dig deep into the depths of our souls if we are to see past another person's conditioned behaviour and know it is not who they really are. To have this mindset of forgiveness is one of the most powerful ways to let go of who we are not and connect back to who we are. When you look at your ability to transform and find true happiness, it is lying in the hands of other people.

The next time somebody has done something to trigger you, choose to see past what they have done, knowing it was not them, it was their conditioned self. Even if they are lost in the illusion of who they are not, stay focused on the truth of who they are. By doing this you are throwing them a rope and pulling them out of hell.

If somebody presents their shit to you does that mean that you have to show them yours? If somebody throws their shit at you does that mean that you have to throw your shit back at them? It does not matter how others choose to act towards you, as you always have the choice to see past the fictitious self that they are presenting, and only focus on their truth. You see how they are your messenger, sent to help you. When you have this mindset, miracles happen, and ugly situations can naturally unfold and blossom into something beautiful. Sometimes people want to show you how much they are hurting, but do not know how to express it any way other than by hurting you. When somebody does something to hurt you, it is still possible to see past your hurt and their hurt, and only focus on who they truly are to reveal who you truly are. You may feel tempted to do or say something and act out what has been triggered, but you don't have to do anything. You can just be with them, listen, and hear what they are really saying. When somebody says, 'I hate you!' maybe they are really saying, 'I hate myself!' and to see past this is the purest form of forgiveness and compassion. This is not only about being kind to others, as when you choose to only see the truth in others you awaken the truth in yourself. What a beautiful practice this then becomes, as way to help ourselves by helping others.

To only focus on the conditioned self of another means we feed it, and this makes it become more prominent and prevalent. When this happens, we are then faced with a decision. Do we keep looking at what we dislike or hate in another and make it who they are to us, or do we choose to see past their past to reveal who they truly are? This can be challenging, but every meeting with another person's conditioned self is an opportunity to relinquish our own. To see past the conditioned self in another means we can truly communicate with that person, from truth and peace. The opposite applies when trying to communicate with another through who we are not. This is then not communication at all, but rather an illusionary interaction between two mind-made identities. This will usually involve defence or attack towards the person that you are communicating with. To transcend this unconscious and destructive way of communicating, and the conditioned version of who we think we are, we must come back to and abide where our light is shining.

THE SPACE BETWEEN

Imagine what it would feel like if you did not need to defend yourself ever again for anything. Now imagine you need not attack anybody again. Allow yourself to sink into the peace situated somewhere in your body. Imagine how great it would be to live this way. Well you can! There is a space that we can occupy that is situated between attack and defence. When we choose to abide in this space, we open the door to our light, we open the door to ourselves, the truth of who we are. When you attack, or defend yourself, you are choosing to be who you are not. The two main components of the conditioned self's survival come through attack and defence and are two sides of the same coin.

What do I mean when I say attack and defence? I am talking about any thoughts or actions towards another that create a limited state of being within yourself and them. The way we feel is always a perfect indicator of whether our thoughts and actions are pure or filled with hate. The energy behind both attack and defence are the same, and both give fuel to the self that we are trying to let go of. Mother Teresa was once asked why she did not attend any anti-war protests. Her answer was, '"I will never do that, but as soon as you have a pro-peace rally, I'll be there.' Mother Teresa knew that by attending anti-war rallies she would only be fuelling the wars. She knew that this kind of defence was a form of attack and chose not to participate. I am sure that there were many people who wanted to do good by going to anti-war rallies, but without realising, may have been giving the wrong energy to them, the same energy that created the war. What did she mean by saying 'as soon as you have a pro peace rally, I'll be there'? There is a different energy behind peace, and by focusing on this rather than attack or defence, we create a space for our light to shine.

I remember when me and my friend Benni lived in a van for three months. We decided to spend one month camping in the woods. We were heading down from Canada and working our way through California. I introduced him to the spiritual hot spot called Mount Shasta. It was amazing to see how I would 'randomly' meet people that handed me pearls of wisdom. This one evening, me and Benni were sat in front of a fire we had made in our usual spot in the woods when a car suddenly pulled in and headed in our direction. We became a little nervous at first thinking that we were going to be told to leave the spot we were camping at. The car came close and stopped next to our van and out stepped a woman. She came over to our fire and sat down with us. Immediately we synchronised into a conversation. We were sharing stories and conspiracy theories when she stopped me as the conversation had become a little dark and heavy. She looked at me and said, "There may be terrible things happening in the world, but no amount of sadness will make a sad situation better. But to come from a place of peace is true strength, and from there you can change yourself and the world." Wow! I sat in silence and allowed what she had shared with me work its way into my being. I knew that being fearful and verbally attacking the problems that I saw in the world was doing nothing other than sending out the same energy that had created them. I realised that my idea of helping to solve a problem was only helping to perpetuate it.

We seem to believe that feeling sadness and crippling ourselves with limiting emotions will somehow help the starving children of the world. This does not mean that we cannot hold compassion for the people we want to help, it means that we start with our own state of being and create change from there.

I believe it is good to know what is going on in the world, but when we choose to adopt a state of anger, sadness, or fear, it is no good for us or the world. All attack comes out of fear, and fear is the most disempowering state we can be in. We can only feel fear when we are identified with who we are not. We feel small and vulnerable, so we believe we need to stay vigilant and attack those who are out to take advantage of our weakness. When we are identified with this fictitious self, we always experience varying levels of fear, and create a defence in our minds to a perceived potential threat. We may remember a conversation that we had with somebody that made us feel threatened in some way. We know we will see this person again, so we prepare a defence in our minds, just in case they try to act the same way. This means that we are locked into the conditioned self, carrying around an unnecessary defence. We are then closing the door to our truth by believing that we need to defend ourselves. The mind does not know the difference between what we imagine and what is happening. It believes them both to be the same. When you prepare a defence to an imagined attack, your mind believes that the attack has already happened. This means that you adopt the state of a victim, which is why you feel the need to defend yourself. Just like trying to pet an injured dog, only for it to attack you, thinking you are trying to hurt it. The dog sees itself as weak and under attack. Even though you are showing this animal love, it will not see it because it thinks it is weak and needs to defend its vulnerability. We are putting ourselves in the same mindset when we believe we need to defend ourselves. We are adopting a state of weakness whenever we are identified with the conditioned self, and thus believe we need to constantly be on guard to a potential external threat. We allow the conditioned self to re-assert itself through imagined threats that we have chosen to believe are true. When we are connected to our light, we have no reason to attack or defend ourselves. We have no reason to even think of defending ourselves from others.

When we prepare ourselves for a potential attack of any kind, it is our defence that ends up being an attack. Without realising it, a fearful society that are all defensive, become the attackers. If we choose to not see the world as dangerous, we would not need to attack through a defence created by imagining that we may be attacked. We are being the very thing that we are afraid of, when we believe that we need to defend ourselves. Imagine how society would look if we all laid aside our need to be defensive in any situation. How would we communicate?

Become aware of the subtle ways in which you create a defence against an imagined potential attack. This attack can come from your husband, wife, boyfriend, girlfriend, mother, father, sister, brother, friend, boss, or anybody who comes into your life. Maybe you are creating a defence against something they may say to you. Maybe you are thinking of a defence against a comment that somebody usually makes that irritates or angers you. You will feel inside how you contract when you are in a state of defence. However, when you drop the need to defend yourself, you are handing your trust over to a greater power, one that eclipses anything that the conditioned version of you can bring.

The only self that needs to defend itself is the conditioned self. And without the need to defend, you are choosing to relinquish your identification with the limited version of who think you are. "But what if somebody accuses me of something I did not do, or what if somebody treats me badly, surely I can use defence or attack?" In between attack and defence is peace. If you want peace, there are no exceptions. This means you can speak your truth without the energy of attack or defence behind it. You just say what is true without the need to disempower yourself. Speaking your truth has a different energy behind it, as it comes from who you truly are. It is not what you say, it's how you choose to say it. When you speak your truth, it is mixed with conviction and certainty. To be at one with your truth means you need not spend so much time in your head thinking of a defence to a perceived attack. You trust that in any situation you have access to all you need. And when you operate from a place of peace, you are always more than equipped for any eventuality. When you no longer use the faculties of the conditioned self, they become obsolete and vanish, along with the self they were attached to. Your sense of self starts to dissolve. Your sense of the conditioned self that needs you to believe in defence and attack to stay alive will then begin to be forgotten, leaving the truth to be remembered. The space that begins to open when you are comfortable without the need to defend or attack shows you who you truly are. With that comes a great deal of strength. You are then free to enjoy life and relax into all situations knowing that whatever happens, you are more than capable of dealing with it.

Situations that are echoes from the past will come to tempt you back into identification with the conditioned self. These situations will mostly come about through other people. When this happens, you must decide who you want to be. Do you want to slip back into identification with who you are not? Or do you want to stand firm in your truth, allow the situations to pass, and deepen the connection with your true essence? How you respond to situations will either invite the same situations to keep coming or dissolve them and the conditioned self. When you respond differently to a situation, you are no longer believing you are the conditioned self. You feel a spaciousness when you are not locked into the conditioned way of being. This is the beginning of freedom as you are staying open and saying to life "ok, whatever happens I'm ready for and ok with" this allows what has been hidden deep within to arise, so it can leave, clearing the way for your truth. To stay open is the acceptance to come back to yourself. The other option is to be closed and in a constant state of attack or defence. This means you are on guard, protecting and acting out what needs to be let go of.

What do you value the most? Do you want pain or peace? Do you want to live your life identified with a false self that lives in fear, or do you want to remember your truth and live with love? This is what it all comes down to: how much you value truth over the lie. Hate always leads to more hate. Fear always leads to more fear, and love always leads to more love. We always have the choice between two options: love or fear. Why is it then we seem to fear love and love fear? We have lost our faith in love and become afraid of having or being it, through the fear of losing it. We have placed our trust in fear, believing this is the path that will work. But fear is not real, and neither is the self that we have placed most of our faith in.

When you abide in your truth there is no need to defend what does not exist. You begin to see what you used to defend was nothing more than a collection of thoughts and emotions that you called 'me'. All thoughts of this limited self come from the past or the future. When we are connected to the conditioned self, it will react in the present based on what has happened in the past. It will also have you believe that the same may happen in the future. This shows where and how the conditioned self operates. It needs you to attack and defend to stay alive. And it uses the past or future to keep you in fear. When we are lost in the past or future through our identification with the conditioned self, our minds are not clear and available for the truth to shine through. To make the decision to stand in your truth means to stay in this moment. The other decision is to wander off into conditioned analytical thinking, allowing your past to regain control of who you think you are. The simple act of being here, whilst choosing to only see the truth in others, means you are choosing to come home.

THE MIRACLE MOMENT

Imagine who you would be without your limiting story of 'I have suffered, so that means I will always suffer'. Without realizing it, we are all telling our stories that have been created through past experiences. We tell our story through how we act, what we do and don't do, and who we are choosing to be in every moment. Are you your past? Is this who you really are? What if you did not have a story? What if this moment was the beginning of the rest of your life? What if your past was nothing more than a thought in your head? Well, it is! Who could you be, knowing that you are not your past, or your story? To live in this moment without the limiting story being told means you are allowing the truth to be told. This moment, right here, right now, is all you need to be free. How? You just decide that you don't need to tell your story any longer. You drop it because it is not you. Without your story, you have no limitations, because all limitations come from the past. The conditioned self is created through past experiences, so when you drop your story, you drop the past and the conditioned version of who you think you are. The reason we find it so difficult to let go of the past is that it has defined who we think we are. We hold onto it as it brings a sense of identity. Without the past, you would have no story, and no self. Would that mean you do not exist? Quite the opposite. It would mean you can see and be your true existence without your limiting story fooling you. To drop your story means to drop your past and drop your 'self'. All you are then left with is a self that has never been stained by the past. You are left with your truth.

This also applies to how we see other people. Do you hold the past against anybody you know? If so, how does this affect your communication with that person? Do you feel an undercurrent of resentment towards them for something they said or did to you? The truth of another person will naturally shine through when you choose not to hold the past against them. When you let go of all that you think they have done and not done, all you are left with is who they truly are. Then, how they act in the present moment is not tainted by their conditioned behaviours of the past. It is more of a challenge to look past how another person acts in the present when you are holding the pain of what they did in the past against them. Holding someone's past against them can turn an insignificant act into something seemingly unforgivable. It exaggerates their smallest act, and your reaction to it. It is then not what they did in the present that upsets you, but rather all the past pain that you are still choosing to hold against them. You can transform any relationship by choosing not to look at them based on their past actions. A freshness then emerges and allows you to see their light.

The reason we spend most of our lives feeling unhappy is that we play out the past in the present and project it into the future. We seldom enjoy the present moment without anything from the past obscuring it. There is a way that we can tune into our truth, and it comes through this moment. When we live as though this moment right now is all that there ever is or was, we are no longer projecting the past into all that we do. We are no longer holding the past against ourselves and others, believing it is who we or they are. It is like being born again in every moment. To live this way means full dis-identification with the conditioned self. Once we do this, we allow our truth to be all there is, and with that comes true happiness.

The window of the present moment is what allows our light to shine into all that we do. When we are not here, experiencing this moment, we are either focused on the past or on the future. Neither the past or future exists, so when we are living our lives out of sync with this moment, we are out of sync with ourselves, and with life. This moment is all that exists, but most of us seem to be trying to find ourselves more happiness, pleasure, and contentment in the next moment. We daydream and fantasise about how great the next moment will be in the hope that it will save us from this moment. Before we know it, we have spent a lifetime lost in the next moment, which never arrived. We say things like, "Maybe the next course will give me what I need to be happy", "Once I have more money I can start enjoying my life", or "Not long now until I retire, then I can start living". We are always projecting our happiness and freedom into future moments. We can be eating breakfast whilst thinking about what we should eat for lunch. We then eat lunch thinking about what we should eat for dinner, and as we eat dinner we can be thinking about what we will eat for breakfast the next day. Amusing as this may sound, we do it all the time, but not just when we are eating. We fantasise about future moments in the belief that they will bring greater satisfaction.

What happens when you start to live in and for this moment? Insecurities and fears dissolve because the truth of who you are is given space to arise. We give so much of our attention to the past and future that we miss the only thing that is real: this moment. This moment is the doorway to who we are.

Without the shadow of the past dimming our view of the present, we can allow our light to shine. Everything we need is in this moment, in the here and now. It's not in the future, its right here. This is what Eckhart Tolle clearly states in his book *The Power of Now.* "Time isn't precious at all, because it is an illusion. What you perceive as precious is not time but the one point that is out of time: The Now. That is precious indeed. The more you are focused on time – past and future – the more you miss the Now, the most precious thing there is."

Our level of happiness is determined by how long we can stay aligned with this moment. When you are truly at one with this moment, with no concept of the past or future, you feel at peace, as there is nothing to be anxious or worry about.

What is it that pulls us away from this moment? What is it that steals our happiness and freedom? It is our conditioned fears and thoughts that coax us away from the truth of who we are. These conditioned fears are part of the conditioned self. The whole point of peeling away the conditioned self is to take away most of its power and pull. This allows us to abide in this moment as the awareness that watches all that is happening. And when something is triggered and shown to us, we can peel that away whilst keeping ourselves in this moment. The strange thing is that people fear being present. To just sit and be quiet and not need to do anything can be a challenging task. We feel afraid of what we might feel by just sitting and doing nothing. Doing nothing may even feel alien to those who have always needed to be doing something. But all this doing is part of the conditioned self's way of distracting you from yourself. It appears doing nothing has become the hardest thing to do. We always must be doing something or trying to get somewhere as though what is here is the enemy. The conditioned self knows that the present moment is where it can be seen for what it really is. It then has nowhere to hide. This is what aids our realisation. "If I don't experience any fear, anxiety, or sadness when I abide in the present moment, that means that the conditioned self cannot exist here!"

How much do you trust living without the instructions of the conditioned mind? Witness how your mind tries to pull you away from the simplicity of just being here. It will say things like 'this is boring, let's check our emails instead' or 'there's nothing happening here, let's find something to do'. A great way to witness the resistance towards being present is to bring it into your conversations. Can you have a conversation with another person with no mental rehearsal of how 'you' want the conversation to go? When you are conversing with another, can you be fully present and listen to every word of what they are saying without trying to think of something interesting to say before they have finished speaking? This may mean that there is silence when each of you have finished speaking. Can you be comfortable with these silences, sit and allow what needs to be spoken to arise, rather that always rushing to have something prepared? You may not have something to say and this is also fine. When you are busy thinking of what you want to say when another person is still speaking, you are not fully present with them. You are somewhere else, deciding what to say rather that listening to what they are saying. This can result in two people who are talking but not really listening to one another. When you allow what needs to be said, rather than preparing something to say, you give space for truth to be spoken. You then feel a deeper connection with the other person, as the conversation moves to a higher level of consciousness. This space of not speaking when we have nothing to say allows us to sink deeper into our truth. We have become more focused on being seen as interesting and making sure we say things that the person we are speaking with will like, rather than allowing the conversation and connection with another to take on a life of its own.

Next time you are talking to someone, notice how you feel the need to jump in and say something interesting before you forget it. Feel the temptation to try and find something to say before the other person has finished speaking. Notice the anxiety and subtle fear that arises when you are allowing silences when you have nothing to say. Allow yourself to be quiet inside and trust that the right thing to say will come. Then notice how what you are saying comes from a different place than the conditioned busy mind.

Another great and simple way to practice being present and connected to this moment is to be aware of your breath.

The slow in and out, up and down movement of your breath happens without any conscious effort on your part. As you go about your day, be aware of this automatic process that is always taking place and keeping you alive. As you bring your awareness to your breath you are keeping your focus in one place rather than allowing the conditioned mind to be all over the place. Your breath is your lifeforce, and by just being aware of this simple act of breathing, you bring the focus away from your thinking and back into the present moment.

The true challenge comes when we are faced with a situation that tests our ability to stay present and not lose ourselves in thinking. You may be hit with a sudden unexpected situation that makes your mind spin, along with heavy emotions. Sakyong Mipham practises and teaches Shamatha Meditation and is the author of the book *Turning Your Mind into An Ally.* He says in his book, "Let's say we're flying in an airplane. In one moment, the flight attendant is serving us food and drink, and in the next the airplane makes a sudden drop. One minute we feel safe, then fear is all there is. Even though the pilot quickly regains control of the plane, it takes us a long time to regain control of our mind. Even when we're safely on the ground, the fear is so solid that we feel nervous about flying again." It is one thing to be here and abide in this moment. But it is a practice to stay here when the onslaught of situations and thinking tempts us to fall back into identification with the conditioned self.

The whole point of meditation is not to try and stop yourself thinking. Resistance against thoughts will fuel them. This does not mean indulging in thinking either. Meditation is more about allowing your mind to do what it needs to do whilst being aware of it. Naturally your mind will begin to settle into a more peaceful and natural state. Just like how emotions want to come and go, so do our thoughts. If you allow your thoughts to pass by without the need to engage with them and lose yourself in them, they cannot affect you. If you are pulled in by a certain thought, the present moment is the anchor for you to come back to. You will then begin to see how the simplicity of just being here in this moment is a miracle. This is what the Indian guru, and spiritual teacher Osho meant when he said, "When you are here and now, sitting totally, not jumping ahead, the miracle has happened. To be in the moment is the miracle." To be here, present, even only for a few seconds brings peace of mind. And the great thing is that it is always available, and just a breath away. Meditation does not mean you must sit with your legs crossed and eyes closed either. You can go about your day and just be here without the need to indulge in meaningless thinking. The breath is a nice reminder to come back to this moment. After a while you will feel a calmness that follows you wherever you go. This calmness and peace is always here and never goes away. It is only ourselves that leave the calmness and peace when we choose to be in our heads, identified with our thoughts, believing they are who we are. Being present in this moment is more than trying not to think. It is having no need or desire to think and allowing your thoughts to pass by. It is putting your trust elsewhere, not in your thinking, knowing that it inevitably always leads to nothing but pain.

The conditioned mind always wants to operate in the past or future, never the now. It dwells on what has happened, is anxious about what may happen, but never fully engaged in what is happening. When we experience true happiness, it has come through our full dedication to what is happening now with no concern for the past or future. We are fully here, and our senses are alive, tuned into the richness of life. We are always able to live this way, but it means letting go of the conditioned self's need to steal our attention and not be fully present. This means learning to trust life without the need to rely on a thought system that is setup to distract you from yourself.

LIVING WITH UNCERTAINTY

How are you ever going to find yourself when you are trusting a conditioned thought system that always steers you well away from who you are? To search for who we truly are through who we are not means we will never remember who we always have been. To no longer trust the guidance of what is taking us back into unnecessary suffering, we must place our trust elsewhere. To live with uncertainty is to exercise trust in the unknown, the unknown being your pathway back home to truth. There can be uncertainty and strong resistance to following the guidance of the present moment, and it can feel like we are learning to walk again. But we begin to see that there is an intelligence at work that is much greater than anything the conditioned mind can conjure up. This intelligence is who we are and is working to bring us back to ourselves. This is why, when we let go of our conditioned thought systems about how life should look, we allow it to be as it is, and to work for us.

To live in alignment with the present moment means to have total trust and surrender to all that is happening. If you are driving and you get a flat tyre, you have two options. You can get out of the car, angry and frustrated, saying things like 'Why did this happen to me now?!', 'What have I done to deserve this?' or 'Why me?!'. This is a decision to go against life and make yourself suffer. The other way to treat this experience is to be in a state of total acceptance. You accept the fact you have a flat tyre and focus your energy on the solution not the 'problem'. Once you have changed the tyre, you get back in your car and carry on driving. You do not have to be happy about having a flat tyre, you just accept what life has presented, deal with it and carry on. You can be aware of the inner voice complaining and choose not to engage with it. You can also be aware of any frustration, or even anger, rising and choose not to identify with it and let it pass. Life will always bring experiences that aggravate the conditioned self, this we know for sure. But, when you stay open and let all experiences pass right through you whilst choosing not to get caught up in any conditioned reactions, you allow the conditioned self to be stripped away. By doing this, you are integrating yourself back into the fullness of life. The only 'problem' is our conditioned interpretation of what is happening, which becomes a veneer over what is truly happening. And just like Shakespeare says, "There is nothing either good or bad, but thinking makes it so."

We can either have a life filled with unwanted situations, or we can operate through life in a state of acceptance until we start to see there are no situations. To be in a state of acceptance totally contradicts the way the conditioned self would have us live. We are never truly living when we follow the guidance of our conditioning. In every moment, every interaction with another and every experience, we are called to drop our illusionary interpretation of what is happening. We are then moving with life rather than against it. We are allowing grace to gently embrace and guide our every action. The feeling of how we move through life then becomes softer, gentle, and effortless. We notice how life becomes incredibly synchronistic. We do this by treating every situation as though we asked for it, because on some level, we did. When you go through life in a state of surrender and trust, your conditioned limitations rise to the surface to try and keep you in a state of contraction and limitation. They will try to make you believe that what is happening should not be, and if you take the bait, you suffer.

Moving with life dissolves the conditioned self, which always wants to go against what is happening. When we start to trust and embrace all that is happening, we allow our transformation to begin. Change can be painful, but only when we resist it. We have become complacent, comfortable, and lazy in our patterns and comfort zone. When change comes along and tries to assist in our peeling away process, we kick, scream, and fight against it. Change can be challenging as we let go of parts of ourselves that we have carried for most of our lives, even aspects we know do not serve us. We can hold onto a part of us that brings nothing but pain. Just like a child who loves his abusive parents, we become reliant on conditioned parts of us that are abusing us.

Letting go of our conditioned self can feel as though we are losing something important, when in fact we are parting with what hinders our ability to truly be ourselves. Once we become familiar with something, it brings a level of safety and even comfort. Suffering can become a safe place, when we have spent most of our life experiencing it. That usual feeling of darkness and loneliness can have an undercurrent of safety attached to it, more safety than the unknown, and so we cling to it. “Even though I am suffering now, could life be worse?” Our need for certainty can be the very thing that makes us hold onto what we are trying to let go of. We may become frustrated with life and want it to look different, whilst knowingly or unknowingly wanting it to stay the same. We have become so reliant on certainty that it has become the driving force in all that we do or don’t do. It becomes much harder to break free from the conditioned self when our conscious search for freedom and happiness conflicts with our unconscious need for safety and familiarity. This can create confusion and disorientation and feel like we are trying to find our way out of a maze blindfolded.

How does this relate to our conditioning, and more importantly not being able to let it go? The quick answer is that to realise and live our true limitless nature can be a daunting prospect when we have limited ourselves for most of our lives. Imagine being completely free of all limitations and conditioned behaviours. Sounds great, right? Well, if it was great and we wanted to fully let go of our conditioned limitations, we would have already done so, and we would be living at one with who we are.

We are afraid of the unknown, so we resist letting go of the self that limits who we are. The reason the unknown can be a scary place is that the conditioned self cannot exist there. Its whole existence is built on needing to know what will happen. This means that the conditioned self will use fear when we are choosing to embrace the unknown. It fears the unknown, where it has no reference point and nothing to hold onto, and the more comfortable we are with not needing to know, the less strength the conditioned self has. The truth is that you will never know what is going to happen, even if you think you know, so why try to know in the first place? The only thing we need to know is that we do not know what will happen, and that everything always works out when we trust in life. You then become expansive to give more space for life to pass through. Life begins to change shape and moves faster with opportunities and abundance flowing in. When we stay in this expansive state, we allow our expansiveness to expand even more until we trust life more than the conditioned mind. We then move with life, trusting the form it takes, and what it is showing us. When we react to a situation that life brings, we are assuming we know better than life. This creates a state of contraction back into the body. With that comes a feeling of pain as we resist life and our true nature. We seem to think that we are these small individuals who must somehow figure out where to go and how to control life to make us feel happy. Does that ever really work? The times that we are truly happy is when we drop our arrogant idea that we know better than life and start to move with it.

When you watch a bird flying on a windy day it hardly moves its wings and allows the wind to do the work. The bird is using the force of the wind to take it where it needs to go. The bird and the wind have become one. You do not see the bird fighting against the wind as though the wind should not be blowing. It accepts and uses the wind to manoeuvre itself. We can do the same, we can allow life to take us where we need to be, and in the process, do little on our own. We trust and allow life, knowing it is happening exactly as it needs to. And just like the bird becomes one with the wind, we become one with life. When life presents situations, we can allow them to be as they are and watch them pass. Rather than trying to change the situation to change the way we feel, we accept the situation and allow how we feel to pass through. You will witness how grace then starts to carry you because you are no longer resisting what is happening. If a bird resisted the wind it would tumble and potentially hit the ground and die. We can work with life rather than working against it. We can trust where life is taking us rather than thinking we know best and trying to go in another direction. Do you want to see situations as something that should not be happening, fight against them, suffer and delay or refuse your transformation into truth? Or do you want to see all situations as an opportunity to come home, back to true happiness? The more we see that life is kind and always trying to help, the more we will accept and allow our awakening to happen with grace and little or no pain. We always have the decision in every seeming insignificant or significant moment to either come home or stay in hell. Michael Singer, the author of *The Surrender Experiment* says, "Am I better off making up an alternate reality in my mind and then fighting with reality to make it be my way, or am I better off letting go of what I want and serving the same forces of reality that managed to create the entire perfection of the universe around me?"

The reason life starts to work when we work with it rather than against it is because we are it. There is no separation, only in our conditioned minds. We can follow the guidance of a fictitious mind-made self that was created mainly through past pain, but it is not who we are. Past pain acts as the catalyst to transform and remember who we are. Then, the tragic events that seemingly ruined our lives and ability to be happy become the only teacher we need to transform our lives and be truly happy. This is because the pain has pushed us beyond it. The darkness has reunited you with the light. And just like the caterpillar creates its own suffering to go beyond it and transform, so can we. We experience pain in the past, hold onto it, suffer, and eventually use it to go beyond it. The pain you experience is there for you to remember and be who you already are.

You can decide right now that you have suffered enough and choose not to engage with the self that makes you suffer. You can also choose to be your true self, the one that is responsible for all your happiness. True transformation comes when you realise that happiness is not the outcome of something you do, but the by-products of who you are. You can then relinquish the need to find yourself, and instead decide to be yourself. You can feel happy right now. Happiness is a choice and so is being yourself. Vietnamese Buddhist monk and peace activist, Thích Nhất Hạnh, says, "There is no way to happiness, happiness is the way." And when we get 'ourselves' out of the way, there is no other way.

HAPPINESS
Excuse me, How do I get to Happiness?
It's Right Here!

ABOUT THE AUTHOR

Richard is a Transformational Coach for men and empowers them to overcome their depression and anxiety.

He believes that our lives reflect ourselves, and once we heal the internal cause of any unwanted health challenge or situation, our bodies and lives naturally heal.

We are then free to reconnect with who we truly are and create a life that is no longer influenced by our conditioned limitations.

To explore the possibility of being coached by Richard or to stay connected with him for upcoming retreats please visit the links below.

Website: emotionalwarrior.co.uk

Facebook: www.facebook.com/richard.sykes.6

Email: emotionalwarrior33@gmail.com

THANK YOU

FOR READING MY BOOK

Your feedback is most welcome.

Please leave me a helpful review on Amazon letting me know what you thought of the book.

ACKNOWLEDGMENTS

Book edited by Catharine Stott

catharinestott64@gmail.com

Book cover by Adam Clare

adamtclare@hotmail.co.uk

Book illustrations by Irwan Kurniadi

www.fiverr.com/irkurniadi

17693502R00115

Printed in Great Britain
by Amazon